It Was Quite a Ride

Bonnie Graham

It Was Quite A Ride

Moving through the Twentieth Century

Bonnie Graham

NORT STAR PRESS OF ST. CLOUD, INC.

St. Cloud, Minnesota

ISBN: 0-87839-341-2
ISBN-13: 978-0-87839-341-1

First Edition, July 15, 2009

Printed in the United States of America

Published by
North Star Press of St. Cloud, Inc.
P.O. Box 451
St. Cloud, Minnesota 56302

northstarpress.com

Dedication

To my husband, Chuck,
and our sons,
John, James, and David

CONTENTS

Introduction

This work has evolved with twists and turns and unexpected new directions much as the pattern of my life. I began with small essays for my family. Then the scope grew as I realized that over the last fifty years I've been in the middle of a landslide of changes, especially concerning women.

The 1960s and 1970s were difficult times on the college campus and everywhere. I felt the buffeting in my own life as I was caught in the dramatic scene, but I was too busy with my family and other activities to try to sort it out. However, I mused often, hoping to make sense of the changing times.

I did quite a bit of writing for my counseling workshops and college classes that provided some underpinnings for this book. However, it was not until the 1990s when I took my first writing class that my thoughts began to unfold. My ideas came out in small essays—snippets here and there. I saw my life's path running alongside the Women's Movement, but in its own unique way. I wrote what I felt, and enjoyed putting my thoughts on paper. Gradually, the idea of a book evolved.

I have to thank my writing teachers in Arizona, Ardith Guest and the late Irene Lassiter. They inspired me.

I could not have done this without my editor, coach, and friend, Jill Breckenridge, and my computer saviors, Steve Strange, Sean Studer, my husband, Chuck, and Geneva Davenport. I am beholden to Susan Szech, our son David's administrative assistant, for making sense out of my edited script and typing it on a disc, and to our son, David, for his willing assistance and support when I needed it. Thanks and appreciation, too, to friends and clients who are a part of this effort.

My love and gratitude to my husband whose fulfilling and exciting career made most of this possible, and whose patience in answering questions and remembering dates kept me on course. I also want to thank our sons, John, James and David, our daughters-in-law and grandchildren, all of whom, to quote Paul Tillich, are "the ground of my being."

1

Remembering

The Early Years

As with all infants and toddlers, it was through the eyes of my mother that I first remember this world. The day I decided to appear, the temperature was way below zero and snowy —an average February day for Duluth, Minnesota. I was born February 16, 1930. My mother and dad had trouble getting to and from the hospital, which was seven miles away on snowy, hilly, slippery Duluth streets. We had to stay in the hospital an extra day because of the weather—ten days in all. Since we did not have a car, we relied on friends for our transportation.

My parents couldn't decide what to name me. Finally, after waiting nine months, they called me "Bonnie" because I was born on Sunday, and "a child that is born on the Sabbath Day is bonnie and blithe and good and gay." This is from an old nursery rhyme. Six weeks later, they named me Florence Yvonne Ure. Florence is for my mother's best friend in college, and Yvonne for a woman my dad knew in France during World War I. I wish I knew more about her, but my dad died before I had the courage to ask him. When I went to school, my mom told the teacher to call me Yvonne.

I must have been a fairly strong-willed child. My mom said I was independent and had a mind of my own. She told me I loved going to the nearby cemetery pond and begged my mother, father, or grandmother to "go see pretty yake and throw rocks—plunk!" I was persistent. I loved my dolls—still do. My earliest memories are of pushing them up and down the street in my doll buggy.

My sister Janet was born September 19, 1931. I don't remember her arrival, but as soon as she was on her feet, we played together. My grandmother lived with us at this time. We called her "Muna." Our off-and-on babysitter was the girl next door. Her name was Philomena. We called her "Mina." We called our mother "Mama," and she said communication got very interesting.

My mother, Kathleen E. Ure, and Bonnie.

I do remember when my sister Kate was born March 15, 1934. Janet and I took one look at her and said, "Let's go play dolls."

In 1933 we moved from St. Paul Avenue, Hunter's Park, Duluth, to Oxford Street on the border of Morley Heights and Hunter's Park. It was during this time that I began to have my own memories.

Kathleen E. Ure and Spencer Ure.

The house was on a hill. It was a two-storied, white-framed house with a nice open front porch, and three upstairs bedrooms. It was cold most of the time. We had a coal furnace in the basement that had to be "fed." My mother and father were continually shoveling coal into the "oven" to keep the fire going. They banked it at night which meant they let it go down but not out. Many nights mom put a hot water bottle, a flat rubber container filled with very hot water and sealed with a stopper, in bed with us. The heat of the bottle warmed the bed at least temporarily.

Delivery of the coal was a big event for me. The truck came up the driveway. Then the driver put a slide down from the truck into our basement. This was called a coal chute. The coal rolled into our coal bin where it was ready for use. I can still remember the smell of that fresh coal!

Our house got so cold one winter that my mom froze her toes standing in the kitchen. In spite of the cold, I loved winter. Maybe it was because that was all I knew. In Duluth we had nine months of winter!

3

We played in the snow a lot, digging tunnels and making snow castles and not having sense enough to come in when we got cold. I froze my cheeks several times. In those days our outdoor clothing was all woolen. No nylon or polyester had been invented yet. We dried our snow pants, mittens, and jackets on racks near the stove or fireplace. Today the damp wool smell still reminds me of winter in Duluth.

I didn't know it at the time, but the year 1936 was a big year for me. It was the year my father became ill and the year I started school. I was six in February and began kindergarten that same month. School was on the half-year then, and students started either in the fall or winter depending on their birthday. I can remember my first day of school well. It is a picture I will always have with me. The wind was blowing piles of snow around and it was minus twenty degrees. My mother bundled me up—hat, scarf wound around my neck, jacket, boots with wool socks, leggings, and mittens. I could scarcely move. She put on her coat and then led me out to

The Ure sisters in 1936: Bonnie, Janet, and Katie in front of the dollhouse made by their father, Spencer Ure.

4

the street and propped me in the snow bank to wait for the school bus. She couldn't stay with me because my two smaller sisters were inside alone. There I was in a wasteland of white hoping to be rescued soon. Luckily the big bus came on time. This is when I first learned I had to rely on myself. I stuck my hand out of that snow pile and the bus stopped.

I went to Washburn Grade School in Hunter's Park. It was a beautiful building situated with woods all around it. It had a large playground and wonderful ice and hockey rinks in the winter. I felt like a very special person going there. I took the bus from our Oxford Street house, but after we moved to 2232 Vermillion Road in the summer of 1937, we all walked to school. It was about six blocks away.

I loved school. Learning to read in first grade was easy. Learning to write with my left hand was a struggle. The new philosophy at the time was not to change left-handers to writing with the right, but my teacher didn't have a clue about how to teach me as a left-hander. I started out mirror writing $\mathcal{N}$ $\mathcal{N}\mathcal{M}$. Finally, Miss Eiche, my teacher, called in a writing specialist from the Duluth Office of Education to help me. It took time, but we succeeded, and I learned to print and write legibly.

2232 Vermillion Road, Hunter's Park, Duluth, Minnesota.

My Father's illness began in the summer of 1936. I was six at the time. My first memories are of a wonderful, smiling, loving man—often laughing with my mother. He would hug us when he came home from work. I looked forward to the warm feeling I got from his being there. Daddy worked hard as a civil engineer for the Minnesota Power and Light Company in Duluth, Minnesota. They were building new electrical substations around Duluth and in Northern Minnesota to supply electricity for the Duluth Mesabi & Iron Range (DM&IR) Railroad, the iron ore mines on the Iron Range north of the city of Duluth, the city of Duluth itself, and the ore docks in the Duluth harbor.

My dad was eleven years older than my mother. He was born March 10, 1895, in Salt Lake City, Utah—the fourth child in a large Mormon family. His grandparents came to Utah via covered wagon in 1849, just two years after Brigham Young settled the Mormons there. He attended the University of Utah, and in 1917, just before his graduation as a civil engineer, he enlisted in the U.S. Army to take part in "the War to end all Wars!" That was World War I.

His unit landed in France in the spring of 1918, and he fought there as an engineer/infantry man in three major battles. He was gassed in two of them. As a gentle Mormon boy, the horror of war was more than he could bear. He told me his best friend was blown apart standing right next to him in the trench. He talked very little about the war but he described fighting in Flanders Field, near Ypres, Belgium, in 1918. This was after there had been battles going on there since 1916 and bodies from those battles were being churned up in the mud.

My mother and father met in Salt Lake City, Utah, in 1928. In 1929 my Father was transferred from the Utah Power and Light Company to the Minnesota Power and Light Company in Duluth. Mom (Agnes Kathleen Eakle) joined him there, and they were married in March 1929.

One night in 1936 I awakened to the sounds of my dad sobbing uncontrollably. I was frightened. Daddy was the bulwark of our family. I couldn't imagine what was happening! I was only six, and even when my mother explained to me that he was suffering from the trauma of his war experiences (reliving them), it didn't make any sense to me. At that age I didn't know what war was.

At that time in the 1930s the doctors called his symptoms a "nervous breakdown," a term that carried a stigma. It denoted a family weakness, something wrong, and it was kept very hush-hush. After his breakdown, my dad spent the next five years in and out of hospitals.

The first was Dr. Gowan's private psychiatric clinic near our home in Hunter's Park. It was a big red brick building set in the middle of a deep dark woods. I thought the place was haunted, and I didn't want my dad to go there. But, Dr. Gowan and his staff were very warm and welcoming, and I was reassured. Besides, my dad seemed happy there. However, Dr. Gowan could not help him. "Shell shock" was a term rarely used in those days, so mom and dad sought other medical help including the Minneapolis Veteran's Hospital. They couldn't or wouldn't help either. My father had signed his discharge papers saying he was in good health.

Since in those days there were no monies available for a veteran unless he was treated in a veteran's facility, my parents were in deep financial trouble. Daddy spent several sessions in Duluth hospitals and then in the winter of 1942 he went to live with his sister, my Aunt Lida, and her husband, Uncle Vincent Benion, on their ranch in Cokeville, Wyoming. He stayed there until the middle of August of 1942. This was where he hoped to find peace. It was during this time I became my mother's "right hand man." We shoveled the driveway and coal into the furnace, mowed the lawn, and fixed everything we could.

I have often thought that a big contributing factor to my dad's troubles were the signs coming from Europe that we (the world) might go to war again. He felt his fighting in World War I was all in vain. He was also distressed that he could not provide for us as adequately as he envisioned.

During the years 1936 to 1941, Daddy worked off and on. The Minnesota Power and Light kept him on a small retainer. It was a struggle to get by. What really seemed to turn the corner for him was the birth of our brother, Spencer McDonald Ure, August 29, 1942. We called him "Mickey." Dad built wooden trucks and trains for Mickey, and the two of them spent hours in our basement playing with their electric train.

My mother's life had been difficult even before she met my father. Her father was a dispatcher for the Santa Fe Railroad. She was an only and lonely child. They moved many times around the Southwest. On several occasions her father left her and my grandmother. She often spent summers in Portales, New Mexico, with her grandparents and aunts and uncles. By the time she was in high school, her father was drinking and living with other women. Her mother, my grandmother, Muna, liked to party, too. My mother often told me, "I felt like the adult in the family."

Mom was the valedictorian of her 1923 graduating class at West High School, Salt Lake City. She graduated from the University of Utah in 1927 with a degree in Education and specifically U.S. Western History.

My mother had learned to cope well with difficult situations. In the first years of my life (1930 to 1936) we were better off economically than many folks during that Depression time. After my father's illness became debilitating, we struggled to make ends meet.

I remember my mother and her difficulties paying the bills. She tried not to bother my father about these things because of his fragile condition. When my brother was born in 1942, I shared my parent's bedroom with my mother. She nursed Mickey at night, and I was a good sleeper. My dad slept alone in my sister's room.

During the years, 1936 to 1941, we received a lot of help from friends and neighbors—especially clothes and things such as second-hand ice skates, a bicycle we all could share, and food. It was a time of community. We all helped each other with what little we had.

My mother and I always were good friends. She was the one who encouraged me in high school to take business courses so I could work my way through college as a secretary. That was what I did. She also trusted me, and I tried hard not to let her down.

My life as a child living on Vermillion Road from 1937 to 1941 was pleasant. My dad's problems were in the shadows for us as children. I have attempted to portray those days with "snapshots" of our life then.

SNAPSHOTS FROM VERMILLION ROAD

Snapshot I: Our Garden and House

My dad working in our beautiful backyard flower garden. I'm certain we had vegetables, but I remember the flowers best—Larkspur, Delphinium, Hollyhocks, Cosmos, Zinnias, and many others. Our garden was a sea of blue, pink, purple, and white. Someone before us had sunk an old bathtub into the garden for a fish pond, but daddy filled it in and planted flowers. One time when he was planting cucumbers, he spilled the seeds unknowingly into his garden brush pile. That August we had cucumber vines in all directions. We picked cucumbers, and mom made endless jars of pickles. Our house smelled of brine for months.

Snapshot II: Playing House with Our Babysitter, Mina

When Mina came, we were transported. She helped us create a new world all our own. We started by taking all the blankets off the beds and stretching them over the living room furniture. We made palaces, castles, houses, and then we created families to live in them. We three little girls were queens for a day. My mother seemed happy that we had such fun, and Mina made the beds before she went home.

Snapshot III: Playing Dress Up with My Neighborhood Girlfriends

We would don our mother's and grandmother's old clothes and be the grand ladies of the day. Our hats were wacky and wonderful. Our high heels and our attempts to walk in them were a riot. There we were

Bonnie and her friend Beverly playing "dress up" in the summer of 1940.

with 1920s and 1930s slim fit dresses stretched over our pudgy bodies. Sometimes my friend's mother would let us sit in their car and pretend we were going on a trip. Many an afternoon, we sat in our living room, listening to *Ma Perkins* and playing Monopoly or Parcheesi.

Snapshot IV: Camp and Swimming

I was nine years old. The phone rang. My mother called to me smiling, and asked, "Would I like to go to summer camp?" I told her I didn't know. "What is summer camp?" She explained to me that it was a place where I would be outside most of the day, learn to swim and boat, do creative projects and be with other girls my age. It sounded wonderful to me.

The camp was Camp Wanakewan, a YWCA camp for girls located about fifty miles south of Duluth. I had been offered an anonymous scholarship for a week's stay. I never did find out the name of my benefactor.

My mother and I took the city bus to the "Y" in downtown Duluth to meet the camp bus. There I met the other girls. My mother left. Although I knew no one, I was happy and excited about this adventure. I loved camp.

My biggest thrill was learning to swim. We used the buddy system, and my buddy and I were placed in the cordoned off beginners area

10

where the water was waist deep. As I recall, neither of us was afraid. After several attempts, we finally managed to put our faces in the water and blow bubbles, then lay on the water face down with arms and legs out, doing the "dead man's float." I felt so proud. Next we used our arms and legs and actually propelled ourselves forward. We were swimming! What a feeling. I remember the blue sky, green fir trees, blue water, and my swimming in all that beauty.

Snapshot V: The Iceman Commeth

When we first lived on Vermillion Road, we had an icebox. An icebox is an insulated cabinet or box usually made out of wood and lined with metal. There was a compartment for food and, along the side, a place to put large pieces of ice. When our ice supply ran low, we put a placard in our window which was visible from the street. It indicated the pounds of ice we would need that day. Soon a big truck came by loaded with ice. We kids saw it coming down the street and ran to meet it. The driver would pick up the ice hunks with large tongs and take it across our lawn and into the house. The ice dripped small slivers—cold and delicious to us. We learned early, though, not to run in bare feet—those slivers cut our feet.

Snapshot VI: Girl Scouts

When I was eight years old, I joined Brownie Scouts. It was such fun for me and good positive reinforcement because we did small projects that I could see to completion. At age ten, I was eligible for Girl Scouts. It is hard to capture what scouting did for me. I loved earning badges. I've always been goal-oriented, and I learned so much as I worked on such badges as Reading, Music, Birds, Government, and Wildflowers, among others. My lifelong love for wildflowers and their environment grew out of searching the woods for the flowers.

Ever since I can remember, the Girl Scouts have had a Girl Scout Cookie sale. Selling the cookies was a great experience for me. I met and visited with the near neighbors and beyond, and I was persistent in selling.

I've always liked earning money for myself or someone else. I won many cookie awards.

Another fond memory of Girl Scouts is of our times at Winter Lodge. Calling it a lodge was stretching the point. It was a large one-room shelter about one-half mile off the road. We had to ski in with our supplies on a toboggan. The first thing we did was to build a fire in the stove. Outside the temperature varied from ten below to ten above. The inside was often just as cold. We kept busy trying to keep warm while the lodge heated up. We made our beds, cooked dinner, sang camp songs and generally enjoyed ourselves. Outdoors we had snowball fights, made snowmen, tried to identify animal tracks in the snow and skied around the area. Our skis were flat boards with the ends tipped up and a strap that went over our overshoes or boots.

Snapshot VII: Whooping Cough

Every life has a turning point, and my contracting whooping cough was one of mine. It was the spring of 1938. I was eight. At first my mother thought I had a bad cold. Then I began to cough and cough. She called the doctor, and he called the City of Duluth Health Officer. The Health Officer came to our house and verified that, indeed, I had whooping cough. He then nailed a quarantine sign on our door. It looked like this:

WARNING
WHOOPING COUGH
Exists on These Premises
Children residing in this house are forbidden to leave the premises without permission of the health officer. The occupants of this house will be held responsible for the unauthorized removal of this car.
By orders of M. McC Fisher, M.D.
Date _____ 1938 By _____

No one could come or go as long as whooping cough resided in our house. My dad was allowed to go to work. That was the exception. Janet got a mild case, but she recovered quickly. After that, she could go to school. Kate had to stay in four weeks to see if she would get it. I was sick six weeks and coughed for months afterwards. I remember standing under a big pine tree in our front yard and coughing until I thought I would break in two. I coughed up buckets of phlegm. It wasn't a pretty sight!

Whooping cough was hard on my lungs. After that, I had many sieges of bronchitis and more coughing. Added to my stress was the fact that my mother, father, and grandmother were chain smokers. I lived in a house full of smoke. At about age thirty-eight, I discovered I couldn't breathe hiking up hill or at higher altitudes. The doctor told me my lungs were, and are, full of scar tissue. He asked me if I liked to swim. I told him I was a water rat, and that was when I started swimming laps. I have been at it ever since. I swim about a mile a week. The exercise keeps my lungs elastic and my psyche intact.

Snapshot VIII: The Turners

Our neighbors on Vermillion Road were the Turners. We called them Mr. and Mrs., but they were Fred and Charlotte to my parents. They were a source of admiration and wonder to me.

Mr. Turner owned the drugstore located about three blocks from us at the corner of Oxford Street and Woodland Avenue. To me, he was a round, medium height, kind man, and very business-like. He never said much. His wife was a take-charge lady. I liked her. She, too, was round but bustling. She made wonderful lemonade. The Turners were managing better during the Depression than most of us. They had a lovely brick home on Vermillion Road across Mygatt Avenue from us.

I was often invited to visit their oldest daughter, Charlotte, who was bedridden upstairs. To visit Charlotte, I entered into the downstairs hallway with the living room on the right and the dining room on the left. The kitchen was behind the dining room. The stairs went up in the middle of the house. Halfway up, Mrs. Turner had a sewing room. I loved that room and the house. It seemed so cozy and homey and perfect!

Charlotte was a mystery to me. I was only eight when I first met her. It was scary going to her bedroom, but she was warm and kind

13

when I got there. She had beautiful dark-brown hair and must have been about twenty-five years old. She looked small and withered in her bed. I found out later that she had multiple sclerosis. Her brain was very good, though, and we talked about what I was reading or our favorite radio programs.

Charlotte had two sisters younger than she. Margaret and Betty were college age at this time. They had movie star clothes; at least that's what I thought. Every once in a while, they would give a beautiful sweater to us—one they no longer used. I remember a soft baby-blue sweater that made me feel like a princess. When the girls cleaned their closets, we got more lovely things.

Snapshot IX: The Fourth of July

The Fourth of July on Vermillion Road was wonderful! After closing the drugstore on July 3rd, Mr. Turner brought home all the left-over fireworks. On the Fourth of July, he and my dad built rocket-launching platforms, and the glory began. My sisters and I were ages eight, six, and four when we first witnessed these wondrous sights. Of course, we had never seen the Big Time, but this was pretty big to us.

One Fourth we will never forget. On this particular night my dad was helping, as usual, and dropped his lighted cigarette into the unused fireworks bag. What happened next was wonderful, frightening and crazy. We ducked down as rockets and Roman candles went off in all directions. My mother tried to corral us into a safer place and keep us down, but we peeked. It was colossal! The fireworks were going both sideways and upwards—a real spectacle! It could have been tragic, but we had no sense of that at the time.

Snapshot X: The Community Chest

All through our grade school years, we collected money once a year for the Community Chest. It was the Depression, and most of us had very little, but we all knew someone worse off than we were. Our donations were mostly pennies, nickels, and dimes, but they added up.

Imagine my surprise when I was invited to represent Washburn School at the big annual Community Chest victory luncheon and present our school's monies. I was in sixth grade at the time. The luncheon was held in downtown Duluth, and I was overwhelmed to be in the same room with the mayor, business leaders, politicians, and church leaders. I was seated next to Margaret Culkin Banning, one of Duluth's prestigious authors. I managed to speak a few words to her now and then. She was lovely. My appreciation of books was greatly enhanced by this encounter with a real author.

Snapshot XI: Reading and the Library

It was in fifth grade that my love of books and authors was solidified. If we'd had a good day, our teacher, Miss Crandell, read to us the last half hour of each day. Most days she read, but sometimes the boys were naughty, and I was furious. Then she made us do homework until the school bell rang.

One of the books she read was *Little House in the Big Woods* by Laura Ingalls Wilder. It was totally pertinent to us. It was set in Wisconsin with the same age children in the story, same big woods and our same climate. After Miss Crandell finished the book, we all wrote to Mrs. Wilder, and she wrote back to the class. We were thrilled.

From about ages twelve to sixteen, I began looking in the adult side of our local library for my reading material. Our librarian was terribly worried that I would find something not fit for a young woman, so she was constantly suggesting books for me. One I will never forget was *I Married Adventure* by Martin and Osa Johnson. It was about Africa, my first taste of the foreign world. What Miss Lillian didn't know was that I was reading *Forever Amber*, a racy new novel, at the time. Word passed among those of us who did baby sitting as to where it was hidden in various homes!

I grew up in 1941. It was a momentous year, challenging and even frightening at times. Four events came together that greatly determined the focus and shape of my life to come.

We moved in May. It was a hard move. I loved Vermillion Road, my neighborhood and friends, but because of my dad's illness, we could no longer afford to live there. Our new house, which we also rented, was in Woodland, about two miles farther out from Hunter's Park. I knew no one there. The young people in that area went to a different grade school.

The trauma of our move that summer was mitigated by one of the most exciting times in my life. Traveling by myself on the train, I visited my grandmother in Salt Lake City, Utah. I was eleven years old. My Grandmother, Muna, said she could afford to pay my way if I came before I turned twelve. My eleventh birthday was in February, 1941. My ticket was a youth rate.

Kathleen E. Ure and "Muna."

My grandmother, Minerva Elizabeth McDonald Eakle, "Muna," with Bonnie in 1931.

On June 23, my mother put me on the train in Duluth. Our former neighbor came to the station in Minneapolis and helped me board the right train for Omaha, Nebraska. In Omaha my Uncle Scott, my dad's brother, met me. We had part of a day together, and then he found the train's hostess, and put me into her hands for the trip to Salt Lake City. She led me to a lower berth and told me my room, car number, and the location of the dining room. The train was the Union Pacific's Challenger that ran from New York City to Los Angeles. It was beautiful to me. I was excited, but never particularly worried. I seemed to have

17

confidence it would all work out. This was the beginning of my many travel adventures.

I was thrilled, fascinated and enchanted every minute of my two month's visit. With my grandmother I took a bus to Amarillo, Texas, and Portales, New Mexico, to visit her family, my great-grandmother and great aunts and uncles. Memories of that trip included being called a "Damn Yankee" in Texas. What did that mean? I knew it wasn't spoken in a kindly manner. This is when I first realized parts of the country were still fighting the Civil War. Another more pleasant memory is of my great-grandmother, a shriveled old lady of over ninety years of age with eyes that still twinkled and a smile that welcomed me.

In Salt Lake City I attended the 24th of July parade and festivities and the Wild West Rodeo with my dad's brother, Uncle Lincoln, and my cousins. The 24th of July was the day Brigham Young saw Salt Lake City from the mountainside and said to his followers: "This is the place"—to settle. I can still remember my first glimpse of the mountains in the early morning, the beautiful Mormon temple and tabernacle, and Great Salt Lake. I was excited about floating in Salt Lake. The salty water held me up. I couldn't sink! I asked my uncles a lot of questions about our family and tried to learn and understand.

Most vivid of all is my recollection of the days spent at my Aunt Lida and Uncle Vince's ranch in Cokeville, Wyoming. I rode horseback with Uncle Vince and helped turn the gate for the irrigation water, located a herd of wild horses, and found tracks in the hard clay and rocks made by the wagons coming overland on the Oregon Trail. Two of my older girl cousins were also there. It was nice to feel connected.

That summer the frosting on the cake for me was getting to spend time with my grandmother. I grew to know, love and respect her more and more.

I returned from my trip the middle of August, just in time to start junior high school. Now I was concerned! In sixth grade I worried about this transition. Would I get lost in the new big building and would I ever see my friends?

I took the city bus to school—every day both ways. The trip was four miles each way, and this turned out to be a providential situation for me. It was at the bus stop and on the ride that I met my new friends. On the very first day I realized we were all scared and confused. One might say, "misery loves company." We faced our new experience together.

East Junior High was a beautiful big brick building located in a lovely birch grove. Half of the rooms overlooked Lake Superior. I felt very special going there. Children from seven grade schools throughout the Eastern part of the city attended East Junior. I soon became accustomed to the class changes every fifty minutes, and I especially liked the variety of experiences. We didn't realize it, but we had to learn to think for ourselves.

One way our junior high days were not like those of most adolescents was the effect of the bombing of Pearl Harbor and the start of World War II.

It was Sunday, December 7, 1941, just after Sunday dinner about 1:00 p.m. I remember my dad standing in the kitchen listening to the radio (no TV then) and looking stricken. He was shaking. He said to my mother, "Kathleen, listen to this," and then we all heard that the Japanese had bombed Pearl Harbor! "Where's that?" I asked. My Dad said, "Hawaii." "Hawaii!"—That was us! I knew at age eleven that bombs came from airplanes.

I was frightened! We continued to listen to descriptions of the carnage from CBS and NBC. Then the local broadcasters from KDAL and WEBC came on with warnings for us. In essence what they said was that we in Duluth were in a very vulnerable spot. We were the second most strategic city next to New York since ninety-five percent of the iron ore the US used to make steel came from the Iron Range north of Duluth and was shipped out of the Duluth/Superior harbor. We must be prepared in case planes reached us! I ran upstairs and hid under the bed.

As I was sprawled out in the dark, I couldn't help but remember the poem my mother used to recite about James Whitcomb Riley's reaction to the San Francisco earthquake of 1906: It is called "When the World Bu'sts Through":

> Where's a boy agoin',
> An what's he goin' to do,
> An how's he goin' to do it,
> When the world bu'sts through?
> Ma she says, "she can't tell
> What we're coming to!"
> An Pop says, "he's ist skeered Clean—plum—through!"
> So where's a boy agoin',
> And what's he goin' to do,
> An how's he goin to do it,
> When the world bu'sts through

Indeed, Duluth did get prepared in a hurry. By evening of December 7 we were in a black-out or as black as we could get on such short notice. There weren't nearly as many cars in those days as today, but I recall drivers were instructed to go slowly and only use parking lights. Also, by that same evening we had spotters on the hills surrounding Duluth watching for airplanes.

In time my curiosity got the better of me, and I went back downstairs. My mother told me of the preparations being made to protect us, and my dad showed us on a map just how far we were from Japan. I felt better.

My father's specific concern was Duluth's energy supply. As a civil engineer for the Minnesota Power and Light Company, all the electricity plants (hydroelectric and coal-driven steam) for the Iron Range and Duluth harbor were the responsibility of the Minnesota Power and Light Company's engineering department. One of the first things MP&L did after December 7 was to build a new coal-burning electricity producing plant on the Superior side of the harbor. My father was in charge of the construction of this project. His friend, Ray Holmes, had a similar position with the Duluth Mesabi and Iron Range Railroad—known as the DM&IR. They were both on top alert during the war years.

From the day of the Pearl Harbor attack on December 7 through the ensuing war years, I knew my world had dramatically changed and would never be the same fun-loving innocent place again. Although we experienced no immediate attack, we worried all through 1942 and 1943.

In my junior high school, we had air raid drills—much like tornado drills today. I especially remember the big evacuation drill in the spring of 1942. We were all sent home and instructed to leave our school as quickly as we could. We were told to fan out along the creek beds, under trees, in people's backyards and behind bushes in order to make our way home without being seen by enemy planes—no matter that some of us lived four miles away. We did this exercise in all seriousness. It took two and one-half hours to get home, but now we knew the route if we should ever need it. I kept wondering, "Why would anyone want to kill us?" I learned at an early age that war was not understandable.

These war years changed our life style considerably. Shipping goods anywhere was difficult and many items were scarce. We were encouraged to grow our own vegetables and harvest fruits such as apples and berries when we could. My dad applied for a victory garden near us in Hartley Field and grew vegetables during those summers. This was the first time the land had been plowed or turned that anyone could remember, and it was full of rocks. No one could get them all out, and our carrots and root vegetables grew crooked. I remember him and my sister, Janet, coming home with his harvest in a big red wagon.

We canned hundreds of jars of produce during those years. The fruit and vegetables were cleaned and then placed in jars which were steamed in a large cooker. Apple season was my favorite. We peeled apples and listened to the baseball World Series over the radio. I remember several times when bears came into our neighborhood and climbed our apple trees. We would find the claw marks on the tree bark.

We also had ration coupons to regulate the consumption of scarce products. Each family was entitled to a certain number according to the size of the family. The rationed items included such things as sugar, coffee, meat, and gasoline. We had plenty of meat coupons, but couldn't afford to buy that much meat, so my mother traded them for sugar and coffee coupons—coffee for my dad and sugar for canning. We didn't have a car. Gasoline wasn't an issue for us. I believe we obtained the coupons at our local public school and/or post office.

The summer of 1944, my dad decided to raise chickens in our backyard/woods. My brother, age two, was his right-hand "man." We girls were indifferent. I remember the small chicks were cute. After that I rarely saw them.

That fall when the birds became "beautifully plump," we sat down to a delicious smelling and enticing chicken dinner. As my father started to serve the meal, my brother looked up with tears in his eyes and said, "Mama, are we eating Blackie today?" There we were all six of us about to eat our baby brother's friend. My mother said, "It is war time. We have to make-do the best we can." Then she took my distraught brother to the kitchen to try to console him.

Our meals weren't always sad. We were and are all talkers. Some meals were hilarious. Sometimes when and if there was a lull at the table, my dad would catch my brother's eye, and then raise his food-laden fork and miss his mouth. Often he would do this a couple of times until we all caught on. He performed most often when we had company! Our oldest son, John, remembers these incidents, and laughing until he couldn't swallow.

During the war most consumer goods were scarce. We sewed our own clothes and knit mittens, hats, and socks. I learned to knit when I was eight. We had to take one-half year of both sewing and cooking in seventh and eighth grades. We complained bitterly, but both have been invaluable to me all my life.

As I remember my young life, I keep thinking of my maternal grandmother, "Muna," born Minerva Elizabeth McDonald. She was an important role model for me. To tell her story I need to fast forward to 1954.

My Grandmother, Muna, was coming to visit us by plane and was due to land in Minneapolis. Chuck and I and our two-year-old son, John, were living in River Falls, Wisconsin.

My brother, Mickey, age twelve, was visiting us. We were to meet her plane at the Minneapolis Airport and drive her to Duluth. I had never described my grandmother to Chuck. I didn't know where to start. I figured he would meet her one day and all would be revealed!

At the airport my grandmother bounded off the plane—all five foot two of her, eyes of blue and blonde curls. She wrapped us in her arms, fussed over John and Mickey and then eyed Chuck and said, "What a handsome hunk of man you have there." Chuck swallowed hard and asked about her flight. "Honey chile," she replied, "I just told the stewardess to get me one more glass of champagne, and I won't need the airplane's wings." My Methodist-raised reserved husband and my brother were shocked. Anyway, who had ever met a grandmother like this?

The trip to Duluth was uneventful. I sat in the back with John and Mickey and off and on my grandmother led us in singing, "East side, West Side, all around the town!" We crossed the harbor bridge from Superior, Wisconsin, to Duluth. It was a beautiful day and we were busily pointing out the sights—the Aerial Bridge, the huge grain elevators, and other sites interesting to Duluthians. Then we started up the hill to our house. Chuck, being a great host, pointed out the Duluth Civic Center—a set of beautiful buildings where we had gotten our marriage license. At the sight of those buildings, my grandmother sat bolt upright and exclaimed, "Oh look! Lawsey Mercy. There is the jail. I remember the night I spent there!!"

Shock spread throughout the car. Chuck almost steered into a fire hydrant. Mickey said, "The jail?" My grandmother was my grandmother, and I loved her deeply but her past was something else. She was in jail because she had been partying with friends in Superior, Wisconsin, (across the bay from Duluth). They tried to cross the harbor on the ice in a car and were taken into custody on disorderly conduct charges.

Muna lived with us a good bit of the time from my birth until I was six when my father "sent her packing" She was supposedly a bad influence on us. My mother was an only child, and this must have been hard on her. I later learned my grandmother had had a very sad life, but I never sensed it.

As a teenager I looked forward to Muna's visits—two weeks every two years. She was a milliner in a large Salt Lake City department store, and that was all the vacation she could take or afford. (A milliner makes custom-designed women's hats—most hats were made that way in the 1940s.)

I will never forget Muna's visit when I was sixteen. This time she asked me if I would like to take her downtown to look around and do a little shopping. I was thrilled to do this until we got on the bus. She wanted to sit in the back. Okay with me. When we got settled, she exclaimed so all could hear, "Isn't this fun?—me and my granddaughter" "Sugah (sugar) in the morning, sugah in the evening, sugah at supper time"—her favorite song. (She was a southerner—born in Tennessee.) She sang with gusto and insisted I join her. She also invited everyone on the bus to sing along. Some did! I was embarrassed and mortified. I sang along with her (softly) for a while until I finally got her engaged in a conversation. Even after that incident, I would have gone with her again. Something about her fun-loving spirit, her enthusiasm and her genuine love of all and everything around her inspired me.

Things weren't always out-of-hand with my grandmother. Along with making beautiful hats, she was an excellent seamstress. She made most of our dresses. Many times she fashioned matching outfits for our dolls made from the dress scraps. The doll clothes seemed like works of art to me and were the envy of all our friends. I remember knitting hats and scarves to complete our dolls' wardrobe.

Muna has been one of the most important influences in my life. She was a very positive role model in many ways. Although born in

McMinnvillle, Tennessee, in 1881, she had a college education. She attended Ward Belmont College, a girls' school in Nashville, Tennessee. It later became part of Vanderbilt University. Muna was very bright. She would recite Shakespeare to us. She was also frustrated. As a young woman she wanted to sing and dance on the stage, but her father wouldn't hear of it.

She wrote to me several times a year—often two liners. "I love you." "Happy Birthday." Those small notes were my life-line to her.

My junior high school days were quite like those of any other adolescent. I continued to maintain a high scholastic average. I worked on our school paper, *The Birch Bark*, and took part in intramural sports, mainly basketball. In those days girls were not allowed to run the full court. It wasn't supposed to be healthy, so I played center. The ball was passed to us (two centers), and we passed it to either the offense on one side or the defense on the other. We had a homeroom team and played other homerooms.

In high school I also played basketball. It was the same setup. We played each other's homerooms but did not leave the school. There were no interscholastic sports for girls.

Here are several Snapshots from my junior and senior high school days in Woodland:

SNAPSHOTS FROM WINONA STREET

Snapshot I: Odd Jobs

The term "odd jobs" was commonly used during my growing years. My parents would say, "Their family survived because he got odd jobs," or "He did many odd jobs." I didn't know if it was a statement of praise or a derogatory term. In retrospect, as a teenager, I, too, lived on odd jobs. The children in our family had no spending money—no allowance. It was all my mother could do to buy groceries and other necessities.

My on-going employment was babysitting. My pay was ten cents an hour whether I was responsible for one or four charges. I was in demand because I could take care of a baby. My brother was born when I was twelve, and I had much experience with an infant. I soon realized that I was not fond of chasing little kids around all afternoon, and, besides, it was not cost-effective for me. "Why take care of four when I could sit for just one non-mobile baby?" There I could settle down and read my book and listen to my favorite radio programs such as *Dr. I.Q., the Mental Banker* and *Your Hit Parade* where the ten top tunes of the week were played.

When I was twelve, I heard about a commercial raspberry grower in Woodland who was looking for pickers in the summer. That was the job for me! I was paid ten cents a pint but could regulate my income by being speedy. The berries were red and juicy, and the bushes a lush green. We had all kinds of requirements about the size and color of the berries we picked. However, I had a quick eye and could move with ease through the rows. Also, I was more persistent than some of the other kids. The happiest part of the job was that I was outdoors.

In Woodland we lived about a mile from Ridgewood Country Club. It was a private golf course on the hill. By 1944 the men were at war and the young boys were working men's jobs at gas stations. We heard there was a shortage of caddies, so my two friends and I rode our bikes to the Country Club and asked if we could carry their bags. The men seemed genuinely glad to see us. They taught us the rules and were very respectful. I often caddied for the president of one of Duluth's banks. I can't remember what we were paid for eighteen holes, but we were tipped handsomely. The few boys that were there were jealous.

Snapshot II: Christmas Eve in Woodland

Snow sparkling and dancing everywhere in the dimmed street lights. No sound.

It is so quiet. It is Christmas Eve. We leave our house about 10:30 p.m. and enter the winter wonderland. The church is about three blocks downhill from us on Winona Street. We walk in the street with snow banks three to five feet high on either side. The snow is squeaky under foot. The years were 1941 to 1950. There are very few cars.

As we approach the church, we hear the sound of Christmas carols pealing out from the organ into the night. It becomes a little louder each time someone opens the church door. I think of myself in quiet Bethlehem, and the organ our angelic music. The service is simple reminding us of the birth of Christ.

It is cold as we head back home. The temperature usually hovers around ten degrees below or above zero that time of year. My mother greets us back home with hot cocoa, and we often find our father down on the floor trying to put together a toy for our young brother.

Snapshot III: The Ice Rink—1941 to 1950

The hub of our social life those years in Woodland was the ice rink, located only three blocks from our house on the grounds of Cobb school. It was flooded in November and stayed frozen until mid April. We lived there after school, Friday and Saturday nights and many Sunday afternoons.

The boys played hockey on their segregated piece of ice, which was surrounded by hockey boards, and we girls spent our time practicing figure skating moves we had seen in our one visit to the Ice Follies. For my sixteenth birthday, I had the thrill of seeing Sonja Henie perform at the Duluth Curling Club. I realized I still had a long ways to go to perfect my figures.

Located on the side of the rink was our warming house, the center of our rink activities. It was a small building about twenty feet by twenty feet with a pot-bellied, wood burning stove in the middle of it. Around the stove was an iron railing to protect us. We used it as a place to dry our wet mittens and socks.

Our hope always was that the boys would stop their hockey

The warming house at Cobb School Ice Park, Duluth, Minnesota, 1942 to 1947. (Painted by Marilyn Sjoselius Swenson, friend and ice-skating pal)

game long enough to skate with us. Once in a while they did. Then they would put an arm around our back, and we would glide around the ice in unison. What a thrill! In college at the University of Illinois I met a fellow who could dance on ice. Then we virtually whirled around the rink to music!

Senior high school began with tenth grade. I entered in 1944 at the age of fourteen. Our school was very large. The students came from two big junior highs in east Duluth. There were a total of 1,100 attending while

28

Winter in Duluth.

I was there including 375 in our class. Duluth Central was located in downtown Duluth. It was (and is) an imposing sandstone building which takes up a whole block. It has always been a Duluth landmark with its 230-foot clock tower rising above the city and the harbor. As in junior high, we took the bus to school, seven miles each way this time.

The problem I faced was taking business and college-prep courses at the same time. The business courses were to prepare me to find a secretarial job that would pay my college tuition. With the help of a very kind advisor I got the job done. However, I had no time for extras such as band, choir, orchestra, or drama. I did work on the *Zenith*, our high school yearbook. This was usually after school.

We felt our hearts lighten in the spring of 1945 when the war with

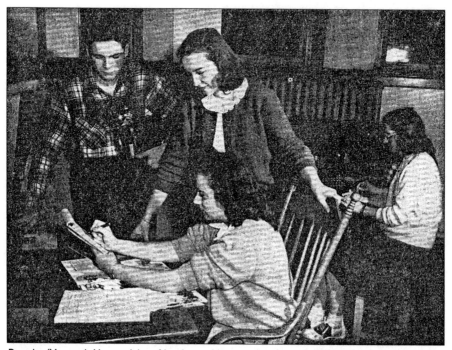

Bonnie (Yvonne) Ure and her friends working on the Central High School yearbook, the *Zenith*, 1946.

Germany finally came to an end. We were ecstatic on August 9, 1945, with the announcement of V-J Day. (Victory over Japan). I was fifteen at the time visiting my friend Caroly Rydell, who lived in Rice Lake, Wisconsin. Her father took us downtown, so we could dance in the streets. We swayed with the conga, high-stepped the polka and sang our hearts out with patriotic songs. It was an experience I will never forget.

Something else occurred to me that night. We had seen a group of blond-haired, blue-eyed German prisoners of war working on the nearby farms. They were not much older than we were. In fact, we thought they were cute. I could imagine how happy they must have been to be going home.

Throughout my high school junior year I continued to keep busy and enjoy school. We were allowed to take physical education electives, so I chose swimming most of the time and, by the end of the year earned my Junior Lifesaving Certificate. My challenge for the year, outside of my studies, was being advertising manager of our yearbook, the *Zenith*. While soliciting ads for our book, I met leaders from both small and large businesses located all over the city. This was the job where I learned that patience and persistence brought results.

I was promoted to *Zenith* business manager in the fall of 1946 when I was a senior. This job consisted of raising and accounting for a yearly $5,000 budget. Consequently, the business staff instigated a rousing subscription drive, three dances, the selling of buttons, streamers, and everything else imaginable. We worked hard and loved it. At class reunions we often have good laughs at our foibles and successes.

The spring of my junior year I was elected into the local chapter of the National Honor Society. I was our secretary my senior year. I graduated ninth in my class.

My social life consisted of working on my various school projects, and attending school events such as football and basketball games, concerts, and plays. We went to an occasional movie, but mostly we spent time at the Woodland Methodist Church. The youth group there was very active. We had meetings and parties in various members' homes, picnics, and a variety of other activities. At this stage in life my friends and I traveled in groups.

I had two individual dates in high school, both to proms. By 1947, there were a few more cars about. One day one of the boys in our gang showed up with a jeep his older brother (a veteran) had bought. We were impressed. He took six of us for a ride, and we immediately headed for the shores of Lake Superior.

Describing Lake Superior is like trying to describe God. I think about "my lake" almost every day. Lake Superior is big, beautiful, powerful, and its grandeur is overwhelming. Moreover, it is hard to fathom because in most places you cannot see the opposite shore.

It is both the largest of the five Great Lakes and the largest body of fresh water in the world, stretching 350 miles east to west and 160 miles north to south. It covers 31,810 square miles and at its greatest depth it is 1,333 feet. When the waves crashed over the rocks, we were impressed and respectful of the lake's power.

From the hillside where my schools were located I could look out every day over the vast expanse of the Lake. When it was blue, it was gloriously blue. When it was stormy, it took on different tones. The drama was provided by the clouds—dark black clouds, clouds with rays of sunshine coming through and rain clouds scurrying across. Many days the Lake was covered by a blanket of fog. With the fog came the fog horn bellowing every few minutes to signal to ships the way into the approaching harbor. The first night of our fiftieth high school reunion the fog rolled in. We were all thrilled to hear the fog horn. We were home!

Lake Superior comes to a point at its westernmost end where Duluth is situated. The St. Louis River flows into the lake there, and the action and force of the river meeting the lake has formed a seven-mile long sand bar or spit called Minnesota Point. We called it Park Point because the bathing beach park was located there. The river has a natural opening on the Superior, Wisconsin, side (the Superior entry) and a man-made canal on the Duluth side spanned by the Aerial Lift Bridge. We crossed this bridge to Park Point. This was our summer playground. Park Point was accessible to everyone because city busses would take us to the very end of the point where the city beach was located. We did not plan to swim in the lake. The water was too cold—never more than forty-two degrees Fahrenheit. We enjoyed the sand and meeting our friends. This was where we headed in the jeep.

My Duluth Central High School graduation was June 8, 1947. It was a lovely ceremony. I did not cry. I was looking forward to starting the University of Minnesota—Duluth (UMD) in the fall. UMD had been Duluth Teacher's College, but it became part of the University of Minnesota the summer of 1947.

My plan to find a secretarial job to earn money to pay my col-

Playing pool at the Duluth Boys' YMCA Uptown Center Club, August 1947.

Youth Center Duluth Boys' YMCA.

lege tuition worked out better than I could have imagined. At the beginning of my senior year, I was approached by my business course instructor who told me the director of the Boys' YMCA, located across the street from Central High School, was looking for a secretary. The hours would be two days after school and Saturdays. I thought it sounded interesting and applied. It was an experience!

I did everything depending on the current crisis. The boys attending the "Y" were from the inner city, ages eight to seventeen. I

33

applied simple first aid to cuts and bruises, broke up or mediated spats and fights and occasionally was made life guard when a substitute was needed. My secretarial work got done around all of this. In the spring of 1947 a new director was appointed. He urged the high school age members to start a youth center in the building that would include both boys and girls. We called it the Uptown Center. The purpose of the club as stated in the Constitution was to provide recreation and a meeting place for the teen-agers of Duluth and to give experience to young people in Democratic planning and leadership. This Constitution was written by Sally Loucks, the first president of the Uptown Center. The following is a description of the center from the *Duluth Herald and News Tribune*, Sunday, August 17, 1947:

> The Boys' Y and teen-age department of the YWCA are sponsoring the experiment, but so far the center, officially dubbed the Uptown Center Club, is standing on its own financial feet. Membership fees of fifty cents per quarter year, plus nominal charges for dances, bring in enough receipts to meet expenses and allow for some improvements.
>
> Currently the club has 170 members. It allows no racial or religious discrimination within the organization. Age limits are fifteen to nineteen years.
>
> By renting the Boys' Y facilities, the club is holding dances, featuring an eight-piece orchestra on the first and third Saturdays of each month, and offers other such activities as swimming, billiards, ping-pong, checkers, and chess. The dances usually attract from 250 to 300 young Duluthians.

I helped with the center both as a youth participant and a Y employee. The orchestra consisted of high school or first year college students most of whom I knew. It was a great place.

By the summer of 1947 I was juggling two jobs. I continued to work at the Y during the school year while at UMD, but was employed in the summer by the Duluth Chamber of Commerce as a secretary to Barkley Schroeder, director of the Tourist and Information Bureau. My "office" was in the lobby of the Spalding Hotel in downtown Duluth. My friend Joan

Bonnie Ure working at the Duluth Chamber of Commerce Visitor Information desk in the lobby of the Spalding Hotel in the summer of 1947.

Otness and I were in charge of the Tourist Information desk. I worked there four summers, 1947 to 1950, greeting 20,000 visitors each year. Every day was new and exciting. We answered questions about Duluth and the vicinity, gave directions to all points in Duluth and environs, planned trips to resorts, and made room reservations in the Duluth area.

Because I could take shorthand, Mr. Schroeder often asked me to sit in on the meetings and record the discussions regarding the economic feasibility of completing the road around Lake Superior and opening up the St. Lawrence River with locks forming the St. Lawrence Seaway, thus connecting Duluth to the Atlantic Ocean. The discussions fascinated me.

Duluth was in an interesting geographic position at that time. Because of the cooling breezes from Lake Superior, we were called the "air-conditioned" city. People would flock to Duluth from Chicago and

35

other hot spots in the summer to cool off. There was no air-conditioning in those days.

We also had many visitors with hay fever. Our cool climate and rocky shores did not allow for the growth of ragweed. It was the only place many of the sufferers could find relief. With the help of the Chamber of Commerce, the hay fever victims formed the Hay Fever Club of America. While in Duluth, they planned many activities to pass the time.

Our problem was finding a place for everyone to stay. In 1947 there were only three modern hotels in Duluth and a few cabin resorts outside of town along the North Shore of Lake Superior near Duluth. A large majority of our visitors stayed in tourist homes. We kept a list at our desk of vacancies and matched it with incoming folks.

I loved meeting the public. Most of my encounters were pleasant, but one incident stands out. That first year I placed an Afro-American physician and his wife in the Holland Hotel. He came back in a few minutes saying he could not stay there. Simultaneously, the phone rang, and the hotel manager began to berate me for sending them a Black person. "Didn't you know that Blacks are not allowed to stay in Duluth hotels?" I did not. I had never heard of such a thing nor could I imagine such a rule existing. I apologized to the couple and found a cabin for them on the outskirts of Duluth along the North Shore Drive. The woman owner of the resort said she didn't care what her other guests would say or thought. She would be happy to have them. It worked out well, but I was almost fired. It was an awakening for me.

My two years at the University of Minnesota-Duluth were happy ones for me. I joined Sigma Psi Gamma, a local sorority, worked hard at my jobs and did a lot of dating. I went with one fellow most of the time but managed to date others when he wasn't around!

My classes were good. Besides my business courses I especially enjoyed music history, sociology, and chemistry. I've often wondered what intrigued me so about chemistry, and I think it was that I could prove something. In high school I almost blew up the chemistry lab because I didn't measure carefully. I probably would have made a mad scientist.

SNAPSHOTS FROM HIGH SCHOOL AND COLLEGE:

Snapshot I: Exploring the Lakes and Woods of Northern Minnesota 1947 to 1951

Whether it was swimming, canoeing, ice-skating, sliding, skiing or hiking, as a young person I lived in the out-of-doors. By the time my college years rolled around, we were mobile. The young men in our group had access to automobiles, and with canoes strapped on the top, we began to explore the northern lakes and rivers. We weren't exactly cautious. I remember standing on the seats at each end of the canoe and rocking until we capsized. It usually was a contest between two or three canoes to see who could stay upright the longest. We also shot some pretty rough rapids.

Mostly we loved the pristine scenery and the quietness of the North Country. The roads along the Gunflint Trail were not paved through the Superior National Forest. We had some rocky rides. Our reward was seeing the wild life—deer, an occasional moose or a wolf.

One day we were at Gunflint Lodge at the end of the Gunflint Trail. We decided to canoe across the lake and have our lunch in Canada. It seemed quite exciting to me at the time. I enjoyed visiting the lodges and resorts in Northeastern Minnesota. I had become acquainted with the owners and managers through placements I made at the Tourist Bureau. We were always welcomed.

Our group usually consisted of my girlfriend, Sally, and myself and our regular dates. We never stayed out overnight. It wasn't done in those days. "What would people think?"

Snapshot II: The Scavenger Hunt on Lake Superior

I have fond memories of some of our escapades along the shores of Lake Superior during our college years. One late winter evening we were on a scavenger hunt. The adventure consisted of groups of us in cars going from place to place in Duluth looking for clues. One clue landed us in a cemetery between the lake and the road. As we alighted from our car, we heard the boom and roar of the ice as the power of the water driven by early spring winds started the ice break-up and the huge ice hunks were thrown on shore. It was scary and intimidating. We found our flashlights and quickly began to search for our clue. Just about the time we found it, the police drove up. They were not happy. We were not supposed to be in the cemetery. It was private property. We said we were sorry and left in a hurry only to find that our next clue took us to the Aerial Lift Bridge pier.

It was dark. The lake was still roaring. The large ice shards were jamming up against the concrete. One could have killed us. We knew that, but reasoned, "If our friends could put the clue out there, we could get it!" We did get it, but once again were stopped by the police. (I don't remember if it was the same officer) The area was clearly marked KEEP OFF. We may have been first to find the treasure. No one can remember.

The next day was brilliant with sunshine and those same roaring ice hunks and shards dazzled like prisms.

The summer of 1948 my Aunt Lenore and Uncle Ernest Carroll came to visit us from Urbana, Illinois. Aunt Lenore was my dad's sister. Uncle Ernest was the dean of the Agricultural Experiment Station at the University of Illinois.

My dream to go away to college had come true. My Uncle teased me about all of my earnings. I told him I would never have enough to leave Duluth and go away to college. To my surprise that fall I received a phone call inviting me to live with them and attend the University of Illionois.

This gave me a chance to move out into the world. I am forever grateful.

2

Getting Started

We met at the Wesley Foundation at the University of Illinois, Urbana, Illinois. It was the winter of 1950. I was a junior, Chuck a senior. For me it was love at first sight. The Wesley Foundation is a student organization of the Methodist Church. In Urbana it was connected to the Trinity Methodist Church (now Wesley Methodist). The church is a large gothic building, nothing like my small Woodland Methodist Church in Duluth, Minnesota.

I walked into the Wesley Hall that cold February day and was overwhelmed. I felt like I was in an old English manor great room. The roof had vaulted beamed ceilings. The small panes in the tall windows were set in leaded glass. Each window and door was surrounded by heavy stone. I thought it was magnificent.

When I finally glanced down to the floor, I saw tables for ten set about the room. I was randomly seated. The people around me were very friendly. But, one stood out. He was on the other side of my table and down a bit. I loved his smile, and asked my tablemate, "Who is he?"

Bonnie and Charles J. Graham at the University of Illinois, 1951.

She answered "Charles Graham, Chuck. He's a senior."

It seemed like an eternity before we went around the table and introduced ourselves. I liked his voice.

We did not converse, but I contrived to greet him again before I left the room. When I arrived home, my Aunt Lenore asked, "Did you have a nice time?" I replied with great confidence, "Yes, I met a very nice fellow, and if he asks me to marry him, I will!" By that time I had dated quite a few men, and I felt like this was Mr. Right.

I heard about the Wesley Foundation through friends I met at the YWCA. They talked about church groups that met on Sunday evenings for supper and a program. (Food was not served on Sunday nights in the dorms or fraternity houses).

I lived near the campus with my Aunt Lenore and Uncle Earnest Carroll. Because I didn't live in a dorm, it was lonesome for me. Coming in as a junior, I had no ready-made group.

I had known since I was twelve that I wanted to be able to support myself when I grew up—no "White Knight" for me! My mother and father were college graduates, but we fell on hard times during the

1930s when my dad suffered "shell shock" from World War I. From that experience I learned that disaster could happen to any family.

In thinking about the future, I ran into a roadblock at my high school. The counselors were constantly trying to steer me into teaching or nursing—admirable professions but not my interests. In high school I had been the business manager of our yearbook, and I thoroughly enjoyed the challenge. I confessed all of this to my father one day in 1946, and he said, "You have as good a brain as any man. Be what you want—an engineer, doctor, lawyer, or business person." What a gift!

In a roundabout way, my father also gave me another gift. At the University of Illinois I applied for and received a LaVerne Noyes Scholarship totalling ninety dollars a semester. This award was given to children of men who fought in France in World War I.

My plan to take business courses in high school to help me find a job to earn college tuition money worked out better than I could have imagined. In Duluth my YMCA job and my work at the Duluth Chamber of Commerce sustained me, and I enjoyed them.

I transferred from the University of Minnesota-Duluth into the College of Business at the University of Illinois in the fall of 1949. By inviting me to attend that university, my aunt and uncle literally changed my life. They opened up to me a new and bigger world. I knew the University of Illinois was a well-known, excellent, Big Ten university. It was a privilege to go there. This is something I could never have done without my aunt and uncle.

At that time, there were 3,000 men and 300 women in the College of Business. We were all "the guys"—no discrimination. The discrimination came when I talked about jobs after graduation, and my advisor suggested that, since I was such a good stenographer, I could get a job as a secretary in a personnel department and work my way up. Upon inquiry, she informed me that the men would start as assistant personnel directors! I call those years "practical feminism." Women accepted this situation because that was the way it was. I've always said I never wanted to be a man, but being a woman hasn't been an easy ride!

Back on campus, Chuck and I dated several times during that spring of 1950. After Chuck graduated in May, he set off on a bike trip to Europe for the summer. When he returned to campus in the fall to work on his master's degree, we began to date regularly.

In February of 1951, we were in a borrowed car parked beside a cornfield near the university campus when Chuck suddenly put his arm around me and said, "Will you marry me?"

I was surprised and not surprised. I had been wearing his fraternity pin since Christmas, signifying that we were going steady. I said, "Yes," without hesitation, certain of my choice. We were both very happy.

However, I was taken back when he went on to explain, "I want you to know what you're getting into. We won't have a very exciting life. I just plan to be a college professor in a small sleepy college town."

Little did I know!

It was the spring of 1951. I was about to graduate with a bachelor's degree in Business Management with an emphasis on Personnel Management. Chuck was to receive his masters in Political Science. We were in the middle of the Korean War, and Chuck was draftable. The good news was that Chuck had been accepted into the doctorate program in Political Science at the University of Illinois and was in line for the Wilson Scholarship, a large stipend for that time.

We did not make plans to marry until Chuck was assured of his grant and was given a draft deferment. We set the date for September 2, 1951. This was just a week before the fall semester at the university. We would be married in Duluth, Minnesota, my home, and then return to Urbana. This we did but not without raising some eyebrows. We wrote our own ceremony, adapted from Richard Niebuhr, unheard of in those days. Fortunately, our minister was a good sport and finally agreed to do it our way. I did not agree to obey! Thus, Florence Yvonne Ure (Bonnie) became the wife of Charles J. Graham. In high school and college, my teachers, professors, and some classmates called me Yvonne. My friends and family called me Bonnie and still do.

September 2, 1951—the wedding of Florence Y. Ure (Bonnie) to Charles J. Graham in Duluth, Minnesota.

We arrived in Urbana a week after our wedding and moved into our rabbit warren of a rental house on Illinois Street. We figured it was built in the 1920s. We were one of four couples and a baby living in a regular three-bedroom, two-story house. Two couples lived upstairs, Chuck and I had the main floor, and the couple with the baby occupied the basement. One of the second-floor couples cooked in the basement along with the couple that lived down there. We had a bathroom in our unit, and there was one bathroom upstairs and a toilet and shower in the basement.

This arrangement didn't particularly bother us. We were happy to have a roof over our heads, and we were used to make-do circumstances. Both of us were Depression babies since I was born in 1930, and Chuck was born May 29, 1929, in LaSalle-Peru, Illinois.

One of our most interesting endeavors in the house was washing our clothes. We had one spin-dry washer and no dryer. All of our clothes had to be hung up somewhere to dry. Most of the time there were clothes everywhere. We had to duck under them or push them aside to stoke the furnace or find the bathroom.

Another interesting experience concerned the garden available to us. One day one of our renters from Canada asked permission to plant some vegetable seeds. She was astounded at their rate of growth. She exclaimed to Chuck, "Here in Illinois you just have to throw the seeds in and jump back." I agreed. She and I both grew up in areas with very poor growing soil and short seasons.

We all still remember the day the neighbor lady brought over a half-eaten cake. She said it had been around five days and her children didn't want any more of it. Maybe some of us would like it. After she left, we all laughed and thought, "Do we seem that destitute?"

During my undergraduate days at the University of Illinois, I worked as a secretary in the Agronomy Department for Dr. Burlison. After we were married, I became the secretary for Dean Howard of the School of Agriculture. I loved that job. However, in spite of modern contraceptives—no Pill yet, less than two months after our wedding I realized I was pregnant. It came as a surprise to me, and I had a lot of adjusting to do. Just two years previously, I was planning to work in Chicago in the personnel department of a big company like Sears. Yet, despite all plans, in nine months I went from college graduate to wife to motherhood.

Since Chuck was an only child, my father-in-law had told me, even before we were married, that it was up to me to carry on the family name. I needed his support, but his reaction to my pregnancy was a blow. Instead of saying, "A grandchild, how nice." he looked directly at me and warned, "It had better not come before nine months." The Graham family reputation seemed more important to him than a grandchild.

Chuck and I had been apart all summer. I, too, hoped the baby would not come before the due date, so I could have more time with Chuck, but early or late was not an issue. It seemed I had stumbled into a generation gap between old and new ways of looking at roles, values, and events involving women. John was born June 7, 1952, nine months and five days after we were married.

A married woman having an unplanned baby was very common in the early 1950s. Many of my friends were in the same position I was. We adjusted and moved on in our new roles. The Pill didn't come on the scene until 1959. In later years, when people asked us about our life before children, we just said, "What life?" In retrospect, we all grew up together. Baby John kept our household lively!

However, before we could settle down as Chuck envisioned, we were off on our first adventure. Chuck was working on his doctoral thesis when he was accepted into a U.S. Management Training Program in Washington, D.C.

Chuck wanted to be assigned to the State Department but because of the McCarthy hearings and other problems, that option was not available. He landed in the Navy Department in the Bureau of Ships. We left Urbana and the University of Illinois in the spring of 1953. In Urbana Chuck was also being courted by the CIA. I didn't know until

45

years later that, when he left the house on some lame excuse, he was taking secret calls in a phone booth or having a clandestine interview. He wasn't interested!

With our one-year-old son, John, we rented an apartment in the Chevy Chase district of Washington. We were a block from Wisconsin Avenue with quick public transportation to downtown. It was another crazy but fun place, much like our Urbana house. We rented the second floor. The Ursells lived upstairs on the third floor. Their family consisted of Erich and Lucile, their three-year-old son, Phillip, and Iona, the Afro-American nanny. They had to walk through the hall on our floor that separated the kitchen from the living room and bedroom to climb the stairs to their apartment.

Erich Ursell was a German Jewish refugee. He had been sent to Britain as a child and, therefore, survived World War II. His family in Germany did not. The Ursells owned a beautiful China shop in Georgetown. We learned a lot from them. Iona, the nanny, who was raised in the South, watched me wash walls, floors, and cupboards in my continuing effort to keep the cockroach population down and declared that this was not work for a white woman.

I had a very special relationship with Iona, but, although I tried hard to change her mind, she would not walk with me on the street. Also, I could not get her to sit at the kitchen table with me and have coffee. Twenty years later when I saw her again, we both laughed and rejoiced that the situation had changed. At Ursell's home in Chevy Chase we ate and drank together.

Our apartment was the best we could do in the very expensive Washington, D.C. Chuck's salary was about $3,900 a year or $325 per month before deductions. The rent was seventy dollars. This compared to fifty dollars a month for a six-room unfurnished house we later rented in River Falls, Wisconsin. The apartment did not have air-conditioning. Had it been a regular apartment, it would have been twice as expensive.

I was born and raised in Duluth, Minnesota, and had rarely experienced temperatures in the nineties until I landed in Urbana, Illinois, and Washington, D.C. My body didn't cope well. I was covered with heat rash and sometimes got light-headed. In order to survive, I put John in his stroller, and we walked over to Wisconsin Avenue to spend at least two hours a day in the air-conditioned Woodward and Lothrop department store and Sears.

Chuck used the Library of Congress to continue his PhD research, and he spent many evenings and weekends there. Other times we piled John into the car and visited historic sites around Washington. We also enjoyed exploring Rock Creek Park located in the middle of D.C.

I learned to drive in Washington. Chuck taught me, and it was tense. He had been driving since he was fifteen and being behind the wheel was automatic for him. Since my family never owned a car, I didn't have a clue about the choke or the clutch. He told me in quick succession to push this or that, and I either did it wrong or not at all. My worst problem was that I'm left-handed and can't instantly tell my right from my left. To save our marriage, we finally hired an outsider to give me a few lessons. After three driving sessions, my instructor pronounced me ready to drive.

My driving test was on Constitution Avenue in eight lanes of traffic! It was a challenge, but I passed. After the test, Chuck went back to work and left me to drive home alone in the heavy D.C. congestion. With white knuckles, I negotiated those infamous Washington circles and five miles of stop signs. I was scared, shaking and trembling, but I managed to arrive home safely. I was twenty-four years old by then and felt very liberated.

Chuck was awarded his doctorate in Political Science from the University of Illinois in October 1955. Along the way, I did some typing for him including the final copy of his thesis which meant one original and four copies. The copies were made with carbon paper. One of the copies was on onion skin, a very fine, thin paper. If I had to make a correction, I had to erase the error on all five sheets and then proceed on. It was a very tough job since there were no Xerox machines then. His finished thesis was 500 pages long.

I did the final typing the summer of 1955. Pregnant with our second child, I told Chuck that I had to get it done because I was getting farther and farther from the typewriter. James Spencer was born November 23, 1955.

Chuck soon realized that the government management training program was not for him. He felt like a small cog in a gigantic wheel. He needed autonomy and more interaction with people. In September 1954 when Chuck received a call from Dr. Walker Wyman, Chairman of the Social Sciences Department at Wisconsin State College in River Falls, to be their first Political Science professor, he jumped at the chance. Finally, we would be in our small college town.

I looked forward to the move. By this time, I was ready for a smaller milieu with a group of close friends and colleagues that were physically accessible. In Washington we all lived in different parts of the metro—no close visiting. I also was happy to know that I would be living nearer to my parents who were in Duluth, Minnesota, only 150 miles away. My father was not well. Seeing him and supporting my mother were important to me. We would also be closer to Chuck's folks in Illinois.

Because the college needed Chuck immediately, we had a month to get moved. We jam-packed our car with our few belongings, mostly baby equipment, and strapped the crib mattress on top. We drove through Hurricane Hazel without even realizing it. We heard on the radio before we left that the hurricane would be coming through Washington, but we reasoned that if we drove west, we would miss it.

As we got into Pennsylvania, the rain began to come down sideways and in sheets. The car, a bullet-nosed 1950 Studebaker, two-door sedan, swayed back and forth. Chuck could hardly keep it on the road, and I felt it might tip over! Finally we stopped at a rest area. The people there said, "What are you doing out on the road in a hurricane?" We were flabbergasted. It seems the storm had veered west. Maybe we were comparing this experience to driving in a blizzard where there was absolutely no visibility.

We waited two or three hours until the worst of it was over, and then drove on. The crib mattress on the top of the car almost blew off a couple of times, and it was ruined. Chuck's parents bought us a new one.

Thus, we began the Togetherness Era.

The Fifties

Togetherness

Togetherness is often used to describe the atmosphere of the 1950s—at least the first part of the decade. With the end of World War II, our men came home. They returned to their wives and children, started new families, and settled down to pick up where they left off. A "return to normalcy" was the cry. Normalcy meant concentration on the family with both parents present, father working and mother home taking care of the children. The word coined for this situation was "togetherness." This concept was so prevalent that the national Methodist monthly magazine was called *Together*. The social pressure to conform was enormous.

My degree from the University of Illinois was a Bachelor of Science in Business Management/Personnel. Since there was a large majority of men in the School of Business, it was not a woman's place. Several of my friends were accountants. Most were educated for a career. We found ourselves in a very interesting situation: what would we do with our talents and training? Our dilemma was the product of a huge schism between idealism and reality. Betty Friedan in her book, *The Feminine Mystique*, published in 1963, called it "the great disconnect."

Reality in 1951 consisted of several new elements in our post-war society. In the first place, women had worked hard in factories, gas stations, and many other industries during the war and proved they could handle home, work, and children.

Second, the factory jobs—in fact all jobs—were becoming easier. Products were being made with smaller and more detailed instruments. By 1951, the small appliance and communications businesses were booming. Often women could do these jobs more easily than men, since women had more dexterity and patience.

Third, the GI Bill allowed millions of young men to go to college. In many cases their wives worked to help husbands with their education. When the husband graduated and became a professional, he and society expected his wife to return home with the kids.

However, through various forms of media, American women discovered that Russian women were doing everything men did. We saw Russian women trained as engineers, architects, physicians, and many other so-called male occupations. For all these reasons, my friends and I got a heady taste of working independence, counter to the pressure to settle down and accept only togetherness.

We moved to River Falls, Wisconsin, in the fall of 1954. The faculty was full of young professors and their families. I had a wonderful group of women friends—all of us with three or four children—mostly boys. This was the small-college town Chuck envisioned. The town had a population of about 4,000, plus 700 students.

It was here I found my lifelong mentor and friend, Helen B. Wyman, wife of Chuck's department chair, Dr. Walker Wyman. As a hostess, she was almost perfection. She was warm, friendly, intellectual and efficient—all at the same time. What was important to me was that she *liked* to entertain. She wanted us to know and support each other. She introduced me to the American Association of University Women, where I found intellectual stimulation, and she gave much-needed support when raising our boys. When I would complain to her about the "antics" of the Graham boys, she would always top my story. She would encourage me by saying, "Don't worry. They are just showing their spunk. They will be fine." And they were.

Helen was a professional in her own right. She taught art in the River Falls High School. In her lifetime, she illustrated several books and was famous for her watercolor paintings of Wisconsin wildflowers.

Walker Wyman became Chuck's mentor. He was a kind, scholarly, very professional person who constantly encouraged the new, young, faculty under him. He left River Falls in 1963 to become the president of Wisconsin State College—Whitewater. Chuck joined him there as the dean of Arts and Sciences.

At this time I got one of my first glimpses into the coming changes in women's roles. Jim was born in 1955. I had nursed John and automatically proceeded to nurse Jim. Many of my friends were horrified. It seemed a nursing woman was considered old-fashioned. Other words used were "peasant" or "contented cow." The "contented cow" syndrome was coined by a woman's magazine early in the 1950s. To quote my friends, "A modern woman wants to be free. She can provide

The Ure children: Bonnie Ure Graham, Janet Ure Olson, Kate Ure Griffith, and Spencer McDonald Ure. Summer of 1955.

bottles so anyone can feed the baby. She will be more sophisticated than her mother or grandmother." I thought nursing was liberating—no bottles to boil, fill or tote around everywhere I went. Besides, I got to hold my babies. Among my friends, however, I was in the minority. I was tied down a bit for three or four months but what was that in the vast scheme of things?

My friends accepted me and my old-fashioned ways, and we got together for coffee, the "coffee klatch," at least two mornings a week. These get-togethers served an almost unconscious need for adult conversation and exchange of ideas, books, politics, and even local news or gossip. We took turns hosting the group. We brought our children along, hoping they would entertain each other, at least for a while, so we could talk.

And yet, I needed more. In time, along with other friends, I joined the River Falls Branch of the American Association of University Women. There we had study groups, meetings with interesting speakers on politics, environmental problems, and other issues of the day. For a while, I belonged to a group studying James Conant's, *The American High School Today*. This was a leading book on problems facing American education at that time. We gathered the kids altogether in one house and hired a sitter for them. Then we met in another house where there was peace and quiet.

Chuck and I also asked a series of college girls to live with us. They baby sat during the day and some evenings in exchange for a free room. That way I was able to get out to attend my groups and occasionally go into the Twin Cities to enjoy a cultural event. We women were all pushing for our own identity and autonomy. The first resident student helper was Jean Biederman from Osceola, Wisconsin. She was a godsend to me, and soon became part of our family.

On the other hand, the students of the 1950s belonged to the silent generation who did not seem visibly upset except about issues regarding race relations. These young people were working hard. They felt they had to make up for time lost during World War II and the

To "my family" with much love, With fear.

Jean Biederman, Osceola, Wisconsin, lived with us at River Falls.

Korean War and to provide a better living for themselves than their parents who suffered through the Great Depression of the 1930s. The majority of River Falls students were paying their own way through college. Most came from small towns and small farms in rural Wisconsin. Chuck used Woodrow Wilson's phrase, "from the ranks of the unknown," to describe them.

To make politics more alive for these students, the campus, and the community, Chuck and several faculty members decided in the mid-1950s to hold a Grass Roots Politics Conference. River Falls is in the far Western corner of Wisconsin and, at that time, people in our area rarely saw a real politician. There was very little television, and only Minnesota stations. The committee invited Wisconsin politicians to give a major speech and then spend time meeting with classes. It became an annual event.

We women enjoyed the events, but one day at an AAUW meeting, someone said, "Why don't we see if we can get some famous women to come for a day each, women who have made a significant contribution to society?"

None of us there can remember whose idea this was. But we all thought it was a great one. We talked about who we could get to come to the hinterlands of Wisconsin. Then someone said, "Let's start at the top and contact Eleanor Roosevelt."

We formed a committee, and the woman who made the suggestion contacted her. To our utter amazement, she said she'd be happy to come to inaugurate our first annual American Association of University Women's Conference.

By this time, Eleanor Roosevelt had worked in San Francisco helping to set up the United Nations, something we all admired. We also remembered her stand against racial discrimination in 1939 when she came to the aide of the famous Black singer, Marion Anderson. Ms. Anderson was to sing in Constitution Hall, which was owned by the Daughters of the American Revolution, the DAR. This organization refused to let her sing there on the basis of her race. Ms. Roosevelt immediately resigned from the DAR and arranged to have Marion Anderson perform a concert from the top steps of the Lincoln Memorial. Thousands came.

To us, Eleanor Roosevelt was the perfect example of wife, mother, professional, and idealistic woman. She came in the spring of 1960 and delighted everyone. She had breakfast with the committee, was very respectful, listened to each woman, and took our members very seriously. Of course, her speech was excellent and the students loved her. I was on the planning committee for her visit but was not there to hear her. The boys and I moved back to Washington D.C. in March 1960 to join Chuck who was working for Senator Proxmire of Wisconsin. I regret missing this opportunity to meet a great lady, but was happy I could be a small part of it.

The next year, AAUW invited Indira Ghandi who had just completed her term as Prime Minister of India. She was followed in 1962 by Pauline Frederick, our Ambassador to the United Nations. After her speech, Ms. Frederick spent several hours in our living room discussing politics and the role of women in politics with our AAUW members, our husbands, and friends.

While we were making these efforts to bring the world to Wisconsin State College—River Falls, the world was coming to us in the form of a cadre of foreign students. Thinking back, it's interesting that they even found us in northwestern Wisconsin. Our big plus was that the Minneapolis/St. Paul Airport was only thirty miles away. I asked an

Zynep Man, an international student from Turkey who was living with us, holding David, age one. To the left is John, again eight, and Jim, age five, is on the right.

Iranian student one time how he found us. He told me that he worked with a person at the American Embassy who was from Wisconsin.

In June 1958, Chuck and I received a very formal invitation inviting us to dine with Mahammud Reza Shah Pavalavi, the Shah of Iran, at an Iranian National Student's Association meeting in Minneapolis. Chuck was the advisor for the local Iranian Student Association in River Falls. The dinner was held at the Leamington Hotel June 27.

The Shah was magnificent. He sat at a table on a level above us. He was dressed in a white Iranian Army uniform with lots of gold braid, and was waited on mostly by women. With a clap of his hand, he would get what he needed. The women would bow before serving his food, then bow and back away. The scantily dressed Iranian women dancers were lovely. They, too, danced on command. With a clap of the hand,

56

the Shah would stop a dance and start another one. He called one woman back for several encores on a clap command.

Chuck and I sat at a ringside table very near the Shah and his party. We knew the dancers and servers were Iranian students studying in colleges all over the United States. I wondered how they fared when they returned to their homeland. In 1958, the Shah was still in favor in Iran, and there was no protesting. In later years, the Shah was considered a tyrant by some, and Iranian students demonstrated against his appearances in the United States.

These many activities took a good bit of my time, but not all of it. I made a lot of phone calls from home, and worked around and among my boys and their friends. Like most mothers of the 1950s, I was at home most of the time. David was born on March 3, 1959. By 1960, John (age eight) was old enough to be a Cub Scout and Jim (age five) and David (age one) tagged along on our excursions. I taught several of the boys to ice skate. After we moved to Whitewater, Wisconsin, in 1962, I drove the Scouts out

Our first house—223 North Fourth Street, River Falls, Wisconsin.

to the glacial moraines to hike and look for fossils. The moraine in Wisconsin is where some of the ice age glacial drift ended. The debris from the drift was deposited there—thus the fossils. A possible lawsuit never occurred to us in those days. Since the boys were about three and one-half years apart, I was a Den Mother for ten consecutive years. I have a medal from the Boy Scouts of America noting this accomplishment and my survival! It was hard-earned, but I had a good time.

We bought our house in 1958. It's hard to find the words to describe how excited I was. My parents never owned a home or a car, and I felt like a queen in my own palace. Our address was 223 North Fourth Street. A local townswoman extended us a personal mortgage at four percent. She did this for several young faculty members. As we recall the agreement was very informal.

Our house was a big older home with four bedrooms, a large living room, dining room, and kitchen. I loved the kitchen. I could put David in his infant seat on the kitchen table, watch the boys play in the backyard, and cook all at once.

Since my talents were in business, decorating was a conundrum for me. I'd never done it before. In my rented family home, we just lived. But, I liked to paint and refinish furniture, so we managed. It is interesting to me that, as a woman, I was expected to have decorating genes and automatically know what would be best and look right.

To quote Chuck, our days in a "small college town" ended with a phone call in January 1960. It was from Ralph Huitt, a Political Science professor on the faculty of the University of Wisconsin-Madison. He had just finished helping Wisconsin Senator William Proxmire set up his office in Washington, D.C. Now the senator needed a legislative assistant. Would Chuck be interested? For a political scientist specializing in party politics, it was like dying and going to heaven.

We moved to Washington in March of 1960. John was in second grade, Jim not yet in school, and David just one year old. Chuck found us a little house in Kensington, Maryland, near the commuter train line so he could get back and forth to the Capitol. It was an exciting time.

By then, Senator Jack Kennedy was campaigning for the Democratic nomination for president. We met Kennedy when he came to River Falls campaigning in the Wisconsin primary. Chuck and others arranged for him to speak on campus. It was early in the morning, and we women were sorry Jackie didn't come along, too. But, I certainly could empathize with her position. She couldn't assume all roles at once—wife, mother, political asset—unless she got some rest and relief. Jack Kennedy was very personable and approachable.

On election night of 1960, we were in the Democratic election headquarters in downtown Washington when the announcement came at about 11:00 P.M. that Kennedy had carried New York. Now we knew for certain that he would be our next president. Pandemonium broke out, and the days of Camelot had begun. In the Senate, Chuck had worked with both Kennedy and Johnson, so we felt very connected.

Kennedy was inaugurated on January 20, 1961. It was cold! We were standing on a thick layer of packed snow, and in spite of my Wisconsin boots and wool socks, my toes, feet, and legs felt like they were turning to ice. But we weren't about to leave. We had "Restricted Visitors" space just below the platform to watch John F. Kennedy being inaugurated the thirty-fifth president of the United States. I was excited about our new presidential choice. I felt we had finally elected someone on our wave length, someone who wanted the average world to be a better place and someone who would fight for civil rights and public housing, someone who would set up the Peace Corp and work for a good education for everyone.

That day, Jackie was beautiful as usual. Robert Frost's poetry was inspiring, but Kennedy's speech was heart-stopping for me. I was one then and an idealist. When he said, "Ask not what your country can do for you but ask what you can do for your country," an electric current ran through me and the crowd. We knew we were hearing history.

In the evening, we attended the Inaugural Ball. Senator Proxmire's wife, Ellen, was in charge of the souvenir favors for the ball. She gave Chuck and me the honor of distributing them at the door. The committee chose gold and silver medallions with Kennedy's and Johnson's profile on them. They were packaged in a nice gold or blue box. Each guest got one. We were at the entrance of the ballroom at the Sheraton Park Hotel in downtown Washington. About 11:00 P.M., Jack and Jackie entered. They were elegant as they greeted the crowd, danced and then left.

I never will forget that moment. But the experience that I think about most often is the one involving my dress. When you are going to a ball, you need a gown. We were very strapped for money in those days, so I wrote to my mother and asked her to send me my bridesmaid dress from my friend Sally's wedding. It was Alice blue, strapless, fit me perfectly, and I loved it!

Imagine my surprise when in the powder room during a break several women began asking me the name of my designer. Did I get it in New York or D.C.? I smiled and told them I purchased it in the Midwest. They were incredulous! I didn't tell them it was ten years old, cost twenty-five dollars, and came right off the rack! It was an equalizing experience for me.

During Kennedy's term, we witnessed the Cuban Missile crisis, the tractors for Cuba debate and the beginning of our space program— plus the start of civil rights legislation and the Peace Corp.

During our stay in Washington, I came to value my friendship with Ellen Proxmire, the senator's wife. She was a bright, intelligent, attractive woman. I admired her, but did not envy her. She came from a close-knit Washington family. Her mother was a school teacher, and her father, who was an engineer/lawyer, worked in the United States Patent Office. Ellen grew up with a strong work ethic. She graduated from Westhampton College for Girls at the University of Richmond in Virginia. The senator, seldom home, worked all the time, nights and weekends, either in D.C. or back in Wisconsin.

This was a second marriage for each of them. Their family consisted of his two teenage children, her two teenage children and their own, Douglas, who was two years old at that time. Their older children spent the summers in D.C. with Bill and Ellen. Ellen juggled her schedule from hour to hour since a great deal was expected of her as a senator's wife. She deserved a break now and then but rarely got one. While we were in Washington, they were invited to a black-tie dinner at the White House—guests of the Kennedys. Bill refused to go. He was all politics. He said he wouldn't go into the White House until he lived there as the president himself. Ellen's situation didn't seem glamorous to me.

I had a little freedom in D.C. because we belonged to a babysitting exchange club. We sat for each other, and the secretary kept a record of the hours we used. We then paid the bank by sitting for someone else. This gave me time to do special things, like lobby for the National Association of University Women at the Capitol and attend special Senate hearings with Chuck.

John was Cub Scout age, and I continued to be a Cub Scout den mother. For the first time, we had an integrated troop. It was a new experience for all of us—both Black and White. I am quite certain it was the first time Black families had been into our White homes and vice versa. We lived on different sides of the railroad tracks—a true barrier. I remember the looks we got as the boys and I walked into the Black neighborhood—skeptical, wary and a few faint smiles. Desegregation was just beginning then.

In John's third grade, Black and White children were also together for the first time. They, too, were wary of one another. John thought the Black boys were too aggressive. I told him maybe that was how they'd learned to solve problems, and said to be patient. The White children had to learn to adjust, too. Our children were trying to overcome more than two hundred years of segregation and prejudice. It took most of the year for the children to come to an uneasy truce.

Chuck and I each lost a parent while we were in D.C. His mother died in Illinois on July 3, 1960. My father passed away after a long illness in December of that year. It was hard for us being so far away. In Chuck's mother's case, I temporarily moved myself and the boys back to Tonica, Illinois, in the spring of 1960. This allowed us to be with Chuck's dad while his mother was in the hospital. John was in the third grade, and Jim in kindergarten. They finished the school year in Tonica.

The small town of Tonica (population 500) was interesting to me. Chuck's dad called me from the hospital every morning. When I went to the grocery store about 10:00 A.M., the clerk would comment, "Sorry your mother-in-law had such a restless night!" Soon I realized that the Tonica operator was listening in on our conversation and spreading the news up and down Main Street.

During that time, Senator Proxmire had many assignments for Chuck in Wisconsin. This allowed him to go back and forth and visit us and his mother in Illinois.

When my father died that December of 1960, I flew out to Salt Lake City for his funeral. It was hard finding someone to stay with the kids until Ellen Proxmire located a very nice nanny for us.

Christmas was hard for Chuck and me, but the boys helped keep our spirits up. John brought home a Christmas tree he had cut on a Cub Scout outing. It was by far the worst tree we have ever had. It was scraggly with uneven and missing branches. It had a crooked trunk, and it listed to the right. It fell over twice, breaking most of our ornaments. John was very proud of it. We all fondly remember it and that Christmas.

Chuck and I made many friends during this time, and we still see some of them today. Many of our weekends were spent with the boys exploring the East Coast especially south of D.C. We visited Mt. Vernon; Jamestown; Yorktown; Monticello at Charlottesville, Virginia; several Civil War Battlefield sites; and Ft. McHenry where the "Stars Spangled Banner" was written. On one of our first trips, we almost ran out of money. We had no idea how many toll roads were involved. Chuck had twenty-five cents in his pocket when we arrived home.

By the time the 1960s rolled around, many of we women were finding ourselves back at work, off to graduate school, running for public office, or starting our own businesses. I believe that our attempt at normalcy that existed before World War II (such as women being home all day and men working outside the home) was no longer normal and paved the way for some of the big changes in society in the 1960s.

Chuck enjoyed his work for Senator Proxmire, researching and writing material for Senate bills, but he was anxious to get back to teaching. We returned home to River Falls, Wisconsin, in August of 1961. It was nice to be back, but it didn't last long. Chuck was appointed the first dean of Arts and Sciences at Wisconsin State College at Whitewater, Wisconsin, in the spring of 1963. Here we met the 1960s head on.

⧼ 4 ⧽

The Sixties

A Testing and Testy Time

T he 1960s were a testing and testy time for everyone. However, the college campus was where the tension was exquisitely felt. The Civil Rights Act of 1964 made it apparent that students of all races were entitled to be in our colleges—live in the dorms and participate on an equal footing. It wasn't just the racial issues that were controversial. There was contention over modern art, women's rights, and the war in Vietnam among other issues.

We moved to Whitewater, Wisconsin, in June of 1963. Chuck was the new dean of the College of Arts and Sciences with 206 faculty members. I was thirty-three years old. He was thirty-four. The boys were four, seven and a half, and eleven years old. Whitewater was a community of about 4,000 townies and 4,000 students located in Southeastern Wisconsin—a very conservative part of the state. When one Whitewater merchant was asked if he had met Chuck, He said, "Yes, but he is a Democrat!" Word preceded us that Chuck had worked for Senator Proxmire.

Chuck's first day in office as dean of Arts and Sciences began with a request from the Art department for nude models. (It was a portent of things to come.) Chuck called his friend, Jim Crane, an artist, who was now at Eckerd College in Florida and asked him for his advice. Jim said, "No nudes is good nudes." Eventually the Art department did have nude models with the disapproval of the community at large, and a new era was ushered in.

A few years later, in 1967, one of the faculty artists submitted a painting to the Chicago Art Institute for its annual show. The painting won second place. Normally and always before, the painting coming in second was hung at the Art Institute but the Institute would not hang the work because of it's subject: it was a large canvas with sixteen small squares. Each showed different phases of the sex act or phallic symbols. The pictures in the squares were not blatant, not fully developed, but the naked eye could get the picture. No one in the administration had known what painting she had submitted. It was a personal choice. Chuck had calls from all over the world about this painting. Most wanted to know what the school was going to do.

The artist hung a black and white version in the Student Center in connection with the faculty art show. The town folks were up at arms. My husband felt it would be better to take it down and told her so, but he didn't order her to remove it. The question for both Chuck and me was, "Where do you draw the line between freedom and decency?"

Eventually, the artist took it down. At that point the Art Department held a protest art burning. They invited the newspapers and television media from Milwaukee and Chicago to watch them burn their favorite paintings—so they said. Later many of these favorites were found hanging in different places around the campus.

In the fall of 1963, we had been in Whitewater about six months. On November 22 I was in the kitchen cooking lunch for Jim, age eight, and David, age four. The beep sounded on the radio and the announcer said, "We bring you a bulletin from Dallas, Texas. The president has been shot." I froze, but my optimistic self said, "They'll get him to the hospital and take care of it." Twenty or thirty minutes later when they told us that President Kennedy had died, I dissolved. His death was not only a tragedy, but it seemed to me to be the death of our dreams. The university was only two blocks away. I called Chuck and asked him to come home. I was sad and frightened, and needed his solace, at least for a while. As Americans and as the world, we lived through the ensuing difficult days, and then began to heal.

In August of 1963, we turned on the television to watch the Black Leadership Rally in Washington, D.C. Martin Luther King was the main speaker. He spoke from the steps of the Lincoln Memorial. This speech was an inspiration to us because King was a Black leader trying, peacefully and with the help of God, to rally the Black people to stand up for their rights. As yet no Civil Rights Legislation had been passed.

In many areas of the United States, very little had been done to establish equality between the races. What we witnessed was King's "I Have a Dream" speech, "where little Black boys and girls and little White boys and girls will walk hand in hand . . ." This was another piece of history that I will never forget. We continued to follow King and his teachings, as hopeful as ever.

During spring break of 1968, our family took a trip to Carl, Georgia, to see Chuck's dad and his wife, Istalena, who were living there. We planned to go on from there to Jeckyll Island, Georgia. We spent the second night of our journey in Evansville, Indiana, just across the border from Tennessee.

While we were eating dinner at a family restaurant, a murmur went through the crowd. "Martin Luther King has been shot and killed!" In the restaurant, at that moment, some people hung their heads, others cried and moaned, and still others cheered. Our sons were sixteen, twelve, and eight. They knew all about Martin Luther King. They were horrified to hear of his death, more horrified to experience the reactions around them.

By the next morning, we knew that King had been shot by a white man. We also knew that we had to drive through Nashville, Tennessee, on US 41 because there was no freeway then and no by-pass around the city. We worried but were not really concerned until we got into the outskirts of Nashville. There we saw people, mostly Black, lining up along both sides of the road. As we neared the center of the city, the crowds grew larger. There were thousands of people, totally silent. We could hardly pass. Chuck said to the boys "look straight ahead, sit up, and do not move." He drove ahead through the crowds as best he could. He didn't think our Wisconsin license plates helped the situation.

We did get through town and proceeded to the Parthenon south of town on a hill overlooking Nashville. As we drove into the parking lot, a police car came up and the officer told us to leave as quickly as possible. He said that he couldn't insure our safety. We left!

The 1968 presidential election was, as our eldest son said, "A horror show." We were saddened by everything we saw on TV. However, we still had hope. We still had Robert Kennedy, John F. Kennedy's brother, who had been attorney general during the JFK years. We were pleased with Lyndon Johnson's "Great Society," but Johnson wasn't running again.

When Bobby Kennedy was shot in that hotel room in Los Angeles, I felt totally defeated. The shock might have been compounded by the fact that we had lost our baby daughter in 1964, adding up to four tragic deaths in five years. The sum of these events affected my dreams, my goals, and my outlook on life.

After Bobby died, I realized more and more that it was up to each individual citizen to do whatever he or she could do to effect change. I hoped we would have leadership, but if we didn't, something could still be done. I began to see that death of dreams can be an impetus for the start of a new dream. I had begun graduate school in 1966 to get a masters in career/employment counseling. It seemed like the thing to do.

With all the killings, I worried about our boys. I felt they might grow up terribly cynical. I heard many teenagers and adults say, "Why try? It doesn't matter what I do." I wouldn't say our sons were angels, but they didn't give up. Each has tried in his own way to augment Civil

Rights, stand up for the disadvantaged, and make the world a better place. I am proud of them.

My personal testing began in January 1964. I became pregnant again with our fourth child and was due in October.

It was a Friday in March when Chuck came home from the college with chills and a fever. He said he didn't know when he ever felt so rotten. By the next day, he was covered with a rash and diagnosed with German measles which he caught from students. The year 1964 was the last time our country had a nationwide German measles epidemic. After that year, babies and children were given measles shots.

My friends said to me, "Thank goodness you aren't pregnant!" I froze! I was two and one-half months into my pregnancy. I could not remember if I had ever had German measles. I knew that I'd had red measles in college and was so sick I missed a quarter of school. So, I called my mother. She couldn't remember which of us had what, but she didn't think I'd had German measles. My doctor gave me large doses of gamma globulin in hopes of preventing my catching the disease. It didn't help the situation that all three boys eventually became ill. I lived in a house with German measles for six weeks.

But I didn't become ill, and by the fourth month, I was confident and optimistic that everything would be okay. Our baby daughter was born on October 11, 1964. She was eight pounds, perfect in every way, but she was stillborn. We were all devastated—the doctor included. He had seen me earlier and hadn't detected any problem except that the heartbeat was a bit faint. He didn't tell me this at the time. Since the baby was turned around, he figured that was why.

Like so many people in this situation, the thoughts and questions began. "Why me, O Lord?" We'd all wanted this baby sister. "Why give her to us and then take her away?" Why wasn't I more suspicious? "Shouldn't the doctor have sent me to a specialist?"

It was determined that our baby's death was caused by strangulation. The umbilical cord was abnormally short, and it appeared that she became tangled up in the last few days as she turned to be born. I asked myself, "Did I overdo those last couple of days?" However, in the final analysis, we found out that she was a German measles statistic. In the year 1964, 20,000 babies were stillborn as a direct result of the mother having contracted German measles during the first three months of pregnancy. I must have had a mild case that was masked by the gamma globulin.

Besides asking myself, "Why me?" I heard expressions from some of those around me that shook my Christian beliefs to the core. Several people said, "It is God's will." How could I believe in a God like that? The greatest comfort I received was from the few folks who simply said, "I'm sorry," or "We are sorry." I gradually began to feel that God was sorry, too, and that God was there to give us the strength to get through the sorrow. I received a gift from God when our first grandchild was a girl. She is twenty-five now and a lovely young woman.

Chuck and the boys were a great comfort to me. One day soon after I returned from the hospital, Jim (age nine) came up to me, put his hand on my knee, looked into my eyes and said, "Anyway, mother, now you can be a Cub Scout Den Mother!" I knew I was needed.

In time I began to wonder, "What next?" I wasn't ready physically or psychologically for another pregnancy. I had always wanted to return to college to take some liberal arts courses—especially history and literature. I never doubted that my bachelor's degree in Business Administration was right for me, but in taking so many business courses, I could not take all the electives that interested me. So, in the fall of 1965, I took a graduate course in the Renaissance and Reformation. My instructor, Henry DeWind, made that era come alive for me, and I came alive, too.

I knew if I was serious about a Master's degree, I would have to decide on a major. One option was a MBA, the other was to become a career/employment counselor. I chose the latter because I loved working with young people, and I could have more flexible work hours to allow time for my family and other obligations. I figured my undergraduate emphasis on Personnel Administration would form a perfect base for Employment Counseling. And it did.

It was a slow go. My life was already hectic. But from 1966 until we left Whitewater in 1971, I took courses, did an internship, and came close to completing my degree.

At one point, I skipped a semester because of other obligations. Our oldest son asked me, "Mother, are you going back to school next semester?"

I said, "Yes," and then quickly followed him into the kitchen. "Why did you want to know?"

He said, "You make a much better mother when you're taking classes."

I thought about that a lot. It's true that when I was busy with my own projects, I didn't and couldn't get all wound up in every "jot and tittle" of their lives. The boys were growing up, and they needed lots of independence.

Running alongside all these various activities of mine, were the tugs and pulls of the emerging Women's Movement. Betty Friedan's book, *The Feminine Mystique*, encouraged women to rethink their lives, to update their education, and look seriously at jobs and career paths.

I didn't have a role model at the time, but I forged ahead anyway, weaving my way between our university schedules, my son's many sports and school events, church obligations, and a myriad of other dates on my calendar. My graduate school efforts didn't go unnoticed by the folks who felt my role was at my husband's side or doing some approved volunteer work.

Chuck was very supportive of me. I did work in our church, help Chuck with many of his projects, and plowed on. All of this activity took time. It took me seven years to get my master's degree (1973), but when I did reach my goal, it allowed me to work for twenty-three years doing what was right for me and, hopefully, to give me an opportunity to help others.

The minister's wife at our church had a tougher time than I did. She, too, was in graduate school, and drove to Madison, Wisconsin, two days a week to attend the University of Wisconsin. This meant she missed many of the women's programs and other church events. In the sixties this was unthinkable. She eventually earned her doctorate, wrote several books, and became a tenured faculty member of the University of Wisconsin at Green Bay.

At this same time, our Methodist church was taking a pro-active stance regarding race relations. We encouraged persons of all races to attend. One Sunday the college youth group, which included several Blacks, put on the service designed to awaken our consciences. The students hung balloons in the sanctuary and then broke them as they discussed our stereotypical beliefs. Some people got up out of their pews and left. The church was in as much confusion as the campus. We suffered through upheaval and growth as did all the churches in the community.

Dealing with the politics of our family, I penned a few observations. In this piece called "Family Politics," I said that I had always lived in a democracy and believed in majority rule or agreement on who is in charge or in power. Add this to the fact that both in high school and college my main interests and majors were business management, economics, and personnel management. When we began to have a family to manage, reality and theory came clashing together. Actually, I think "family management" is an oxymoron.

The struggle for power in a family starts when the baby comes home from the hospital and cries day and night—not on a schedule. Later, the parents agree to do thus and so and the two-year old stomps his or her feet and says, "No." It doesn't get any easier after that.

Raising children presented a first-class dilemma to us. We wanted to give the boys leeway to make their own decisions—to be able to take care of themselves as they matured, but we realized that children needed direction along the way. Furthermore, we had to live together in some sort of family society while this maturing was taking place.

Our oldest son, John, was a master contrarian. He had his own verbal view on everything. The power struggle was constant. Most of the time we had to hold to our decisions. For example, John couldn't bar-

gain out of going to school or the dentist. However, we learned to negotiate with him. Often he would argue with us for hours and then do it
our way. We let him do it his way as much as we could.

On the other hand, our second son, Jim, had his own ideas, too.
He operated in a very different manner and may have done the most politicking of all. He was in the middle and had to work both brothers and us.
He was sweet, silent, and very strong willed. He would ask for something
several times, smile sweetly when I said, "No," and do it anyway. He was
hard to punish, but got into so much trouble doing it his way that he
brought on his own punishment. For example, he was fascinated with the
city dump and forbidden to go there. He went anyway and received several serious cuts. They dampened his enthusiasm, but only a little.

Punishment was a problem for us. I learned early on that the
same punishment for the same crime (fairness) didn't work because each
child takes the penalty meted out very differently. One day I announced
that the next time I heard a boy using bad words and calling names he
would have to put a nickel into the Sunday School Contribution jar.

Sure enough in a day or so John called Jim a "dirty rat." I told
him to get his nickel. He argued with me, said he was saving it for something special, then reluctantly fetched it and put it in the jar. Later that
week Jim used the same offending words. I gave him the same orders.
"Get your nickel." He skipped off, jauntily returned with a dime and
announced, "Now I can call him that again!" Jim was about six years old
and money was of no importance to him.

Sibling rivalry ran rampant. The boys competed with each other
for power and vied for our attention. It was mini-politics at its most vir-
ulent. One day David, age seven, rushed up from the basement. He said
he needed a sandwich for John's lunch. John was thirteen at the time. I
told David to tell John to fix his own lunch. He returned to the rec room
but was back up in just a few minutes wanting John's lunch. After the
third time, David was so distressed I helped him make John a sandwich.
(In retrospect I should have investigated the situation.) It wasn't until
twenty years later while sitting on the front porch of our cabin that the

truth came out. John had told David, "Get me my lunch or I will blow up the house with my chemistry set." Now that is power.

The boys vied for a place in our family society by choosing and excelling in activities that were just the opposite of each other. John played football and ran track. He liked History and Political Science. Jim's forte was cross country. He also played hockey. He became a scientist-veterinarian. David was our basketball star. He later went to Divinity School and then to Law School. I've often thought sibling rivalry isn't all bad. It forced our kids to become themselves.

Running a household takes a lot of organization. In our family we were constantly jockeying for position based on needs—the needs of growing boys (more autonomy), needs of a mother in graduate school, needs of college entertaining and attending college events, and the needs of a father/administrator. I struggled to keep some sort of order. I thought, forget "Management by Objectives." It was more like, "Management for Survival." Communication was our coping tool through all of this. We may have shouted at times, but we talked, bartered, negotiated and tried to say what we felt.

Some of my rules were fairly authoritarian. This was more power than democracy. For example, I got tired of the boys saying to me, "Mom, I don't have a clean shirt" or "Mom, my basketball shorts were supposed to be washed by tonight." So be it. I answered that I would wash anything that was in the wash basket, but I would not crawl under the bed to find clothes. I told them to think ahead and plan. It worked, sort of. Later on they all learned to wash their own clothes and sometimes some of ours.

The dinner table at our house was a study in politicking. John and Jim could not sit together without fighting. David was neutral. We usually sat with Chuck at one end, John at the other, David and Jim on one side with Jim nearest Chuck. I sat on the other side nearest the kitchen. One day when Chuck and John were arguing, Jim said, "I feel I am sitting in the generation gap!" We had the same arrangement in the car. I usually sat in the back seat between two of the boys who were not getting along at that time. The most often repeated phrase was, "How would you like an Hawaiian punch?" The son not involved at the time sat in front with Chuck. I got to drive once in a while. It was a relief.

The summer of 1973 our family politics underwent a sea change. John was twenty-one years old, six feet, two inches tall, and had just returned from a year studying in India. Jim was eighteen years old, six feet, one inch, and had come home after a year as an AFS student in Brazil. During that year David (age fifteen) had grown to six feet, four inches and had become very accustomed to being an only child. It was amazing to see the boys arrange and rearrange their relationships with each other and with us. At this time we began to live as a family of five, mostly grown-ups.

Today we have expanded to three sons, three daughters-in-law and ten grandchildren. We are still politicking but Chuck and I try to stay out of a lot of it. Now it is our turn to say, "No," if it doesn't suit our plans.

Meanwhile, life continued on the campus. In 1967 my husband and his staff set up an Upward Bound program for potentially college-bound African-American students from Milwaukee, Racine, and Kenosha, Wisconsin, and the Native American students from the Menominee Reservation north of Milwaukee. This program was part of the Higher Education Act of 1965 established just after the passage of the Civil Rights Act of 1964.

At that time, Whitewater was an all white community, and this was the beginning of the racial tug-of-war played out in our local churches, businesses, and the university campus. Not only were there difficulties between Whites and Blacks, but the Native Americans from the reservation and the Blacks from the cities had little in common.

Like so many events of the sixties, things happened we could never have anticipated. We were naive. We housed all the participants together in one dorm as a single program unit. This seemed very logical.

One morning we were informed that many of the Upward Bound Native American students were out on the lawn. They had been sleeping on the lawn because they had been told by the Black students there was some sort of voodoo in the dorm. Chuck, the dean of students, the program director, and the student counselors (all White) had the job of convincing the Native Americans to return to the building. There was a terrible lack of cultural understanding on all sides, and a lot of educating to be done.

One night, the African-Americans had to be bussed out of town because of threats by some fraternity members and townies. I am quoting here from a piece written by our son who was a Whitewater High School senior at the time:

As Jake's '63 Chevy pickup slid around the traffic circle towards me, a sharp gust of wind tugged at my coat. I was closing the top button when Jake and Harry pulled up to the curb in front of me. My stomach knotted and twisted into a ball like a bird's nest of fishing line. Rolling down the driver's side window, Jake leaned out, eyes excited.

"Coon huntin' tonight," he shouted. "In town!" added Harry.

Jake drove off to park and headed into the long, flat modern high school. Coon huntin', Christ. Well, my Father was right. They had to get those Black and Indian students out of town before things got out of hand. I hoped that they were on a bus to Madison. This was not the time for police investigation. The fact that one of the Black students had been beaten silly by the Delts, punishment for talking to a White girl at last night's college basketball game was irrelevant. No time to argue your corner guys, just get out of dodge.

Staring into the black hole that was my locker, I felt my body sag. The fatigue of a night of answering calls at the homestead had left a desert of grit where my eyes should be.

75

Covering for my parents while they negotiated a safari to safety with the police, the program administrators and a couple of sleepy, cranky bus drivers was eating into my ability to function. It had been a long night.

The bus arrived safely in Madison.

In time, the university and the community adjusted. The Upward Bound program continues today, and Whitewater is a fully integrated university serving students, not only from our inner cities and small towns, but from countries all over the world.

Whitewater in the 1960s was sometimes a three-ring circus. Along with the issues of race and women's roles, came the increasing crisis on campus regarding the Vietnam War. We had marches, rallies, and picket lines blocking the entrances to classrooms. To handle all of this, there was a police guard at the president's house and the National Guard on campus from time to time. At one point, one of our friends asked if the boys and I would like to move to the country for a while. I said, "If the protesting students come to our house, I'll smother them with kindness, invite them in, give them lemonade and cookies, and then talk with them." Later, I would do just that when student protesters came to us from New Mexico Highlands University. But that's another chapter.

Whitewater is on a diagonal line between the University of Wisconsin-Madison and the University of Chicago, and from time to time the "Chicago Seven" would stop by when they were going to and from these campuses to incite some action from our students. The Chicago Seven were political radicals accused of conspiring to incite the riots that occurred during the Democratic Convention in Chicago in 1968. At this time they were protesting the Vietnam War.

Once again our family was tested. By 1969, our oldest son, John, was seventeen and would soon face draft age. I didn't understand the war anymore than a lot of people and feared he would have to go. On the other hand, I could see that tearing up the college campuses wasn't helping anybody. The protesting made the dialogue to stop the war more difficult.

Our students formed picket lines at strategic points around the campus. Most of us had to cross a line to get to class. There were days when some professors would join in the protest and missed teaching their classes. I was upset when my professor didn't show up. I had paid good money (and spent my precious time) to take that class, and I felt the professor should be there.

To give an idea of life in the classroom at that time, I've included a piece I wrote called:

The Marriage Contract

It was the fall of 1969. I was in my fourth semester of graduate study. Times were crazy on our campus—student protests, picket lines, the National Guard on duty from time to time. Worst of all, I was thirty-nine years old studying alongside the "don't trust anyone over thirty" crowd.

I was just finishing my required courses, the last one being a Grad/Undergrad course in "Marriage in the Family." Here I was married eighteen years, mother of three sons, and part of the establishment. I tried not to argue with the students. They were full of idealism, and I was full of realism, but our next assignment totally intrigued me.

Imagine my surprise and amusement when the professor said, "We'll spend some time today discussing pre-nuptial marriage contracts—not money but 'duty lists'—who does what after marriage." As my Jim would say, "There you have it!"

I thought about my situation for a while and then, instead of producing a list, I decided to tell the class two stories:

The phone rang one recent afternoon. The voice on the other end said, "Is this Mrs. Graham?—Tonight is the night we will be coming over."

"Just a minute." I said. "Who are you?"

"This is Jim Campbell," he said. (Someone I had never heard of.)

"What do you mean, come over?"

"Mitzie is ready, and we need to do it tonight."

"Okay" I said, "and who is Mitzie?"

"Don't you know?" he replied. "We're breeding your Boston Terrier with ours. The boys arranged it."

"I'm sorry." I said. "We can't do it tonight. Chuck is out and David is at Boy Scouts. I'm here alone."

"That's okay, we'll put both dogs in the basement. They'll know what to do!"

I looked at Prince. I wasn't sure about him! All he knew about was getting into trouble. Maybe he would like this kind of trouble. Mr. Campbell, who I finally realized was the parent of one of David's friends, mentioned the contract again and said their female dog was in heat and had to be mated now! He assured me that he would stay in our basement with them.

I was naive. To make a long story short, the dogs didn't have a clue. I ended up holding Prince and Mr. Campbell held

Prince, our Boston Terrier.

Left to right: James, David, and John Graham holding Prince, 1966.

78

Mitzie while they did their thing. It worked. Mitzie had four lovely pups, and David got the money from the sale of one of them. Where would you put this little effort on the "duty list?"

The next story I told was about the first year we were married when I was about seven months pregnant. I was working full time and getting along okay, but I was tired after a full day. My legs ached. I didn't mention this to Chuck. One night I set out to wash the floor after dinner. We were expecting company over the weekend. He said, "Let me do it. You can hardly get down, and, besides, the baby will drag!" I was so surprised! He continued to help me with household chores until well after the birth of our son.

We got to talking about this one day, and Chuck said, "My mother was ill and bedridden from the time I was five until I was eight years old. My dad did almost all of the housework. And I told Chuck that my dad fell ill when I was age six, and much of the time from the time I was six to twelve, he was in a hospital or recovering at my Aunt and Uncle's ranch in Wyoming. He suffered terribly from "shell shock" and gassing during World War I.

I continued. My mother and I shoveled coal and snow, carried groceries because we didn't have a car, and fixed anything and everything we could. My mother had taken a course in high school called Household Physics. This was to satisfy a science requirement. She wasn't very happy about the course, but it helped her immensely in later life. She had learned to do simple electrical wiring and even a little bit of plumbing. I didn't inherit her talents.

I concluded by saying that marriage should be a cooperative effort with lots of flexibility. The students were quiet when I finished. They continued with their lists determined to have equality in a marriage. Maybe they gained a little perspective from my experiences, maybe not.

The professor was smart! Willingly or unwillingly the exercise that day opened the gates for some wonderful discussions in subsequent classes. We all participated—men and women, young and old. I grew to love those students. They were all trying, as I was, to make some sense out of the new social mores of the 1960s.

In the fall of 1968, we were asked to escort a group of Wisconsin State University students on a study tour of Russia. There were 150 American students in all from the seven Wisconsin State Universities. Chuck was the group leader and responsible for thirty students from Whitewater and Superior, Wisconsin. We were gone three weeks. A retired couple from our church stayed with our boys—seventeen, fourteen, and ten. They got along well with our sons.

Students and faculty alike took a course winter quarter of 1969 in Russian history and culture. The tour began right after that at the end of March. It was an eye-opener for our young Americans. These were some of the same students who had been in the middle of the recent campus unrest.

In Russia we were watched and followed and controlled like nothing any of us had ever witnessed. Before we left the United States, the State Department gave us travel rules. One rule was not to take pictures of Russian airports, railway stations, or large buildings. We were also told to always ask permission before taking pictures of Russian citizens. Furthermore, we were warned that if we were arrested for any reason, the U.S. government couldn't guarantee getting us out. We were in the middle of the cold war at that time.

The State Department also told us that if one of us was caught taking off-limits photos, everyone's film would be confiscated. One young man did take pictures at the Leningrad Airport. We were furious and the whole group backed us up when we made him stop. He continued to take forbidden pictures and seemed to feel that Russian rules didn't apply to him. Later, toward the end of the trip, he took a picture of a lady selling eggs on the street without asking her permission. He was jailed, and our Intourist guide informed Chuck of his fate. It was almost noon when this happened. Chuck asked her what the next step should be. She said, "They will release him to you at any time." Chuck waited until about 4:00 P.M. before going to the police station. The student was a chastened fellow after that. His friends weren't a bit sorry.

In Leningrad and Moscow our students were able to spend time with Russian university students. The Russian students weren't allowed to read Western books or study any other form of government except Communism. They knew very little about our Democracy. In a literature class we visited, the students were studying Lenin's version of Tolstoy's *War and Peace*. During our trip, I met and was able to visit with many Soviet women doing non-traditional jobs—jobs often not yet being done by U.S. women in the 1960s. Some of their careers were those of doctor, architect, brick layer, and engineer. I also spent hours talking with our female guide who had children the same age as mine. We soon discovered mothers are mothers the world over. We have the same dreams and problems. We wanted a good safe life for our children. No more war.

Despite the surveillance and other difficulties, our students seemed to have a good time with their Russian friends at Moscow and Leningrad universities. We were immensely impressed with Russian art in all of its many forms. We visited and saw the Hermitage in Leningrad, the Kremlin and the crown jewels in Moscow, the Bolshoi Ballet, the Kirov Opera, the Circus, and the Great Gates of Kiev. I have often thought of the juxtaposition of all that beautiful art thriving and surviving under such a totalitarian, restrictive regime.

We were in Moscow the last days of our trip. Each day our rooms were entered and inspected. One day I found a young maid trying to put on my make-up. She was so sweet. I showed her how to do it and then gave her most of my supply.

Another day when we were lost on the subway system, a gentleman in a trench coat came up to us, announced he was the KGB (like our CIA) and helped us find our hotel. Actually this happened several times. Since we couldn't read the Russian alphabet very well, we often got lost. The KGB was always close by.

As we boarded the SAS airline for Denmark, there was a great sigh of relief, and when the pilot announced we were leaving Soviet air space, the students cheered. To quote the students, "It was a sobering experience!" Freedom took on a new meaning for them.

By the time the summer of 1969 rolled around, we were all ready for a family vacation. My mother lived in Salt Lake City, Utah, and we made the trek from the Midwest to visit her every few years. That year John was seventeen, James fourteen, and David ten.

On the way home we kept the radio on in anticipation of our astronauts landing on the moon. Excitement was building. Would they be successful? So much was unknown.

We found a motel room at Little America near Cheyenne, Wyoming, and settled in—glued to the TV. Just before it looked like the landing would be successful, the electricity went off. Doors flew open. There was a howl all up and down the walkway. This was historic. We couldn't miss it! Within minutes a motel staff member ran up and down the area announcing that the TV was on in the main lobby. The management was using a generator. We jammed ourselves into the small lobby—about fifty of us.

Together we cheered and clapped furiously, and were awe stricken as we heard Neil Armstrong speak and then saw him actually walk on the moon. After the landing, someone in the room started singing "America the Beautiful," followed by "My Country 'Tis of Thee." We were one American patriotic unit that memorable day.

On a cold winter evening in 1970, Chuck and I and friends were sitting in our living room visiting. We had just returned from an evening out to dinner. All of a sudden a glow appeared in the sky in the direction of the campus. Next, we heard fire trucks. Then came the phone call, "Old Main is on fire!"

Old Main was the original very large building on the Whitewater campus. It was built in 1868, and housed the Art Department, the Music Department, the registrar's office, the alumni office, and many other campus services. Many student and faculty records were kept there. The fire was a conflagration. It had obviously been set, since it started in several parts of the building at once. When we arrived, students were standing in front of it cheering. The fire turned out to be a Vietnam War protest. I cried—the waste and futility of it all. John came home from his date. He stayed with his younger brothers while we spent most of the night on campus. He was distressed but never said much. We were all having a hard time.

Chuck had to find a new home for the Art and Music departments. Both needed and required considerable space. Their paintings, art supplies, musical instruments, and general supplies suffered a good bit of damage but were not a total loss. Chuck's biggest problem was keeping the faculty members from rushing into the wreckage to rescue their lives. You couldn't blame them!

There was a grand jury investigation of the fire. Many faculty, students and town people were called to testify, including Chuck. Nothing came of it. To this day no one has been charged.

The fall of 1970, Chuck was invited to apply for the presidency of New Mexico Highlands University in Las Vegas, New Mexico. He was subsequently appointed to the position starting July 1, 1970. Our family liked the idea of moving to the West. That's where I had my roots. However, once again I was a naive optimist. I thought it would be quiet there.

There was trouble from the beginning. The Hispanic students didn't want a Gringo (White). The shoe was on the other foot now because we were the minority. Las Vegas, New Mexico, located sixty-six miles east of Santa Fe on Interstate 25, is in the heart of "Old Spanish" territory.

The student body was forty percent Hispanic, fifteen percent Native American, a small group of Afro-Americans from Chicago—recruited to play football, and the rest White students, many of them from the East Coast. The retiring president was also from the East. He tried to make Highlands the Harvard of the West. He wouldn't allow any Spanish to be spoken on campus by anyone, not even maintenance workers. There was a lot of resentment.

The board thought Chuck had the tools to help the school—such as knowledge of federal programs for minorities, ability to speak some Spanish, and experience implementing campus diversity programs such as Upward Bound.

As soon as Chuck's appointment was announced, letters began to arrive from New Mexico—both pro and con—but mostly telling us not to come. Then a student delegation from the college arrived on our doorstep. They had been sent to explain to us why we shouldn't have decided to come and to encourage Chuck to withdraw. Interestingly enough, the group included one Black, three East Coast White students, and one Hispanic. I invited them to visit on our porch and served them lemonade and cookies. They began to relax. By the time they left us, I think they were beginning to feel that Chuck might be right for them.

The Board wanted Chuck to stick it out. They were certain the students would come to like and trust him. I was, too. What we didn't realize was that, since the color of our skin or nationality can't be changed, it doesn't make much difference what we can or will do. Now we knew what it felt like to be denied access because of race or color.

After the students left, the newspapers in New Mexico took up the cause. The *LaRaza*, the radical Hispanic group in the Southwest hired William Kunzler, lawyer for the Chicago Seven, to lead the protest. However, we did get a letter from the Native Americans saying they were for us.

I was worried about our kids. Jim would be a sophomore—tall, blond and blue-eyed. I was even more concerned when the college called and said we would have to move into our house under cover of darkness for safety's sake.

Two events brought all of this to a head. I received a "blood letter" saying "All Gringos Must Die." A blood letter has drops of blood at the top that run down the page and form a circle of blood at the bottom. I didn't want to interfere with Chuck's decision, so I didn't show him the letter at first. I finally got too worried, couldn't sleep, and was feeling sick. At that point I handed Chuck the letter. He called the police and they called the FBI because it was a threat across state lines. The FBI took my letter, and I never got it back. I didn't even get to copy it. About this time Chuck's contract was taken to court. Without community and campus support, he withdrew.

This whole episode was written up in great detail by Collin Trillen in the *New Yorker* magazine, March 3, 1980.

I was relieved. I no longer had to worry about safety issues for our family, and I wanted to finish my master's degree. Graduate credits were hard to transfer.

We took a two-week vacation in August, and then stayed on at Whitewater where Chuck taught Political Science during the school year of 1970-1971. That same fall of 1970 John entered the University of Wisconsin-Madison as a freshman. He announced that he had signed up for a co-ed dorm (radical concept for 1970). When I questioned him about this, he looked me right in the eye and said, "But, Mom, I never had any sisters. I need to learn about girls!" What could I say?

John enrolled right after the bombing of Sterling Hall, and there were remnants of tear gas on the campus. I was very uneasy about leaving him there, but this was what he wanted to do. He thrived in Madison.

In the spring of 1971 Chuck assumed the presidency of St. Cloud State College, which later became St. Cloud State University, located in St. Cloud, Minnesota. I was so pleased. We were moving back to my home state. I was also apprehensive. The Vietnam War was still on, and I worried about life on the campus. I hoped the War would end soon.

The sixties and early seventies saw old mores and ideals tested at all levels—more freedom of expression in art, new roles for women, the anti-government, anti-war protests and the struggle for racial equality. In many cases, it was "out with the old and in with the new." Tensions were high. Everyone was testing the limits and getting testy doing it.

A sustaining factor throughout these years was a cadre of wonderful friends, several very concerned Methodist ministers, other faculty members and, of course, our own family. We still see our sixties friends regularly. They are rocks for us. This group includes Sue and Jim Schlough, Ruth and John (now deceased) Prentice, Margaret and Dennis Rohrs, Lois and Paul Lauritzen, Vi De Wind, and Bobbie and Noel Richards.

During these years I tried to maintain my balance and sanity by spending time with Chuck and our family, writing papers, doing the work required for my classes and getting lots of exercise—swimming laps and ice skating. I also spent time reading recreationally. I was into Russian authors at that time, and they transported me.

Not long ago, I sat with a group of my friends in a women's discussion group at our church. We meet often to discuss the assigned books we've read, to support each other, and to talk about our roles as women and the issues that confront us each week. In the context of discussion one younger member, twenty years younger than I am, said, "I think the sixties was the most important decade of the twentieth century. I'm proud I was a student then. We finally saw some change."

I agreed with her about the change. She went on to say that the sixties turned the country around. I was tempted to add that the sixties also turned the country upside down!

5

The Seventies

A Decade for Women

The seventies were a time for many new ground rules after the big changes of the sixties. Although sometimes small, gains were made on all fronts. The Vietnam War was concluded in 1975. The Twenty-first Amendment to the Constitution was adopted in 1971. This gave all persons eighteen and older the right to vote and have a say in the government.

Following the Civil Rights Act of 1964, students of all races were entering our colleges in increasing numbers. But to me, the group that made the biggest gains in the 1970s was women. Women began to go back to work—many to renew their careers. Others went to college, technical schools, or other forms of higher education to prepare for a new direction for their lives. Women often left unhappy or abusive marriages. Those already working began to ask for higher pay and equal status. And, women faculty members wanted an equal chance at tenure.

We arrived in St. Cloud in June of 1971. At that time, St. Cloud and the surrounding cities of Sauk Rapids and Sartell had a population of about 40,000. The campus, with close to 10,000 students then, is situated on the Mississippi River in Central Minnesota. Two excellent Catholic schools, St. John's and the College of St. Benedict are located five miles away.

One of the first glimpses of life at St. Cloud came a month or so before we actually moved there. We were invited to the annual May Bowle held at St. John's University. It was sponsored by civic leaders, faculty and staff representing the three local colleges. The benefits were used to support the arts in the three schools. It was a formal dance with over 400 people attending. The colleges took turns hosting the dance, and that year was St. John's turn.

When we entered the Great Hall, we looked up to see a very large Jesus presiding over the congregating party crowd with one hand to the right and the other to the left. On the main floor, under each hand, was a bar! We Methodists were impressed! The mixture of folks there was also impressive: town business and professional people, faculty and staff from all three universities, and guests from all over the area. I began to relax.

The Minnesotans I knew in Duluth were a fairly open and tolerant crowd politically. Party members on both sides seem to respect and even enjoy each other. Hubert H. Humphrey was from Minnesota. At one of our first Open Houses in St. Cloud, I marveled at finding the chairman of the Republican Party's Sixth District and the chairman of the Democratic Party's Sixth District standing in front of our fireplace talking to each other.

In the move, there was one big glitch for me. I had worked hard to receive permission from Whitewater to take my three remaining elective courses at St. Cloud and transfer them back to Whitewater so I could receive my master's from there. However, the registrar at St. Cloud State said I had to pay out-of-state tuition. It was state law. I knew what the duties of the president's wife would be whether required or not. I planned to gladly give what time I could to the college, but I felt, in exchange, I should be able to take the classes free or at least pay only in-state tuition. Chuck went to bat for me with the State College Board, and I paid the Minnesota rate.

Later in the seventies when I got a job in Career Planning and Employment counseling, I worked hard to promote credit changes. Since their husbands were transferred again and again, women were moving around a lot. They found themselves with college degrees half finished and no recognition of the credits at their next institution. Most had to start over. Some never finished. It was wasteful and frustrating. Some changes have been made, but the system still isn't perfect.

Our actual moving day was June 30, and it was hot. I made a million trips up and down our stairs showing the movers where to put our furniture. In the late afternoon, I met a college student helper coming down the stairs with some large boxes. He asked me if I wanted the boxes saved. Before I could answer, he also inquired, "What is your husband going to do in St. Cloud?" I replied that he was the new St. Cloud State College president. The student said without hesitation, "Keep the boxes!"

Our home at 9 Highbanks Place was one-half block from the Mississippi River and one block from campus. We purchased our own home because at that time the State College Board did not provide housing for its college presidents. It was a 1920s, two-story, half-timber stucco house with a big first floor. We had plenty of room for entertaining. Best of all were back stairs leading from the kitchen to the second floor. Our boys could come and go as they pleased and never be noticed. We had four bedrooms, one very narrow 1920s garage, and an equally narrow driveway with concrete walls on both sides. The saying was that the Grahams had to come home sober.

At the end of that first afternoon, we were met at the end of our driveway by two friendly, yet concerned faces. They were our neighbors, the Swansons. Margery had a pie in her hand. Bayliss, her husband, extended a hand to Chuck and welcomed us. Before we hardly said a word, Margery asked, "What do you intend to do about the lilac hedge?"

We looked up. The lilac hedge sat on the grass on the top of our driveway's concrete wall that divided our two properties. It stretched for about seventy feet. We hadn't realized that we owned it.

89

Our home at 9 Highbanks Place, St. Cloud, Minnesota.

When we had time to look around, we saw that the Swansons had a screened-in porch across the side of their house—the side facing us. The distance from our house to their porch was about fifty feet. They lived on their porch in the summer. The hedge was both their shade and privacy.

After we got to know them better, we teased them by threatening to cut down the hedge. Of course, we never did. Bayliss pruned it periodically and every time we heard loud expletives, we knew that he had cut the cord of his electric trimmer again.

Today, we still don't know who owned that hedge. On moving day, we certainly had no plans for it. We were just trying to get moved and get Chuck started on his new job. After we assured them, they relaxed, smiled and joined in helping us. That was the beginning of many lilac hedge stories during the ten years we were neighbors.

Bayliss and Margery were both from Pine City, Minnesota. He is Norwegian and she, Swedish, both proud of their heritage. Bayliss, a pharmacist and graduate of the University of Minnesota, owned one of St. Cloud's largest drug stores. Margery owned and ran the gift shop. She was a Carleton College graduate, and she never let us forget it. We spent ten years debating the public/private education issue with Margery. They have four children. At the time we moved next door, Margret was seventeen, Peter was sixteen, Mary was nine, and Lisa was seven. The ages of our boys

90

were nineteen, sixteen, and twelve. As parents we were facing a decade of teenagers. Little could we imagine the fun we would have.

Not long after our move it became apparent the Swansons had a problem on Monday night. The girls in the household liked to watch *Little House on the Prairie*, and Peter and Bayliss wanted to watch football. Those were the days of one TV per household. Peter came through the hedge looking for a cookie, or some other excuse, to see if our boys were watching the game. Someone usually was, and Peter joined them. Soon Bayliss would follow, and before long, Monday night football at the Grahams became a tradition. I often watched with them. One night in the late seventies, Bayliss and I realized we were the only ones watching. The kids had grown up and all of them were in college or elsewhere.

One day, about the second year of our life at 9 Highbanks, Mary Swanson came pounding on our door screaming that Lisa was stuck in the clothes chute! It was Saturday and Chuck and I were both home. We ran to her rescue.

Margery had stepped out for a few minutes leaving Mary in charge. We couldn't see Lisa, but we could hear her sobbing between the walls. She was about eight years old and was small for her age. The chute was between the first floor and the basement. I ran downstairs to look up and try to assess the situation. I could see both legs sticking down. Chuck saw from the top that she was facing sideways with one arm up and the other arm down. She was definitely stuck. As I tried to calm Mary, Chuck said, "I'm going to get Jerry Weyrens," a close-by neighbor. "He used to be a farmer, and he probably has had experience birthing a calf."

Jerry was home. A miracle! He assessed the situation and asked

Lisa and Mary Swanson dressed in the clothes John sent from India, 1973.

91

The Snow Lady at 9 Highbanks Place, late 1970s.

me to round up all the cooking oil I could find. Luckily, I had a good supply. Then he carefully poured the oil down on Lisa and asked her to move ever so little, if she could. When Jerry felt she was thoroughly coated, he began to carefully rotate her and ease her downward. She slowly slid into my arms.

Lisa emerged from the chute frightened but not hurt. I took her and the sobbing Mary upstairs to clean up. Mary was scared to death because she was supposed to be caring for Lisa. About this time, Margery came home. Her response, after hearing that Lisa was okay was, "Thank goodness you didn't call the fire department. They would have wrecked my house!"

Our Jim and Peter Swanson went off to Carleton College as freshmen in the fall of 1974. Margret Swanson was already there as a sophomore. We hired a U-Haul to get all the kids and their stuff there. The next spring, Jim and Margret showed up with a reconstructed old van. We believe it was in Margret's name. I know we didn't license it or insure it.

At this time Jim and Margret were an item. As parents we were trying to get used to a modern romance. The van was called Herbie. The kids used it for several years to tote gear back and forth to college and for canoe trips. About the time the van first appeared on our street, Molly Weyrens showed up at our door. She was a darling neighbor girl about eight years old. She was writing a neighborhood newspaper and wondered it I had any news for it. All I could think of was that Jim and Margret were home. She happily went to talk to them and begged to see the inside of the van. When her paper came out, the leading story read,

"Jim and Margret have a van with a bed in it." Molly's mother, Mary, with a broad smile on her face, made copies of the paper for all of the neighbors. It was certainly topical!

Not all events involved the kids. From time to time we crossed through the lilac hedge to check on each other's houses when one or the other were gone. One long weekend, the Swansons were away. It was our turn to keep an eye on their house. We went back and forth twice a day to let out their two dogs and check on things.

On the last day of their vacation, we had to be gone ourselves for a couple of hours in the evening. Just before we left, we checked on their house. Margery and Bayliss returned before we did. As soon as we drove up the driveway, Bayliss rushed out and announced, "It's a mess over here! One of the dogs is missing, and all of our silver has been stolen!" We were dumbfounded, but we helped them out as best we could. Chuck found the lost dog hiding upstairs. The Swansons called the police, and we were questioned. What could we say? I began to think out loud how I could help them replace their lovely heirlooms when Margery said, "I didn't know what I was going to do with all this stuff anyway. I'll take the $20,000 insurance money and buy something new I want!" After quite a long time the police said, "Was anything stolen at your house?" We hadn't even looked. We tore through the lilac hedge to find everything in good order at our place. From time to time, I still offer to buy Margery some old silver that she never wants.

With only one boy at home, we thought the Christmas of 1973 would be a quiet one. John and Jim were both overseas. Jim was in Brazil as an AFS student, and John was studying in India through a University of Wisconsin program. About a week before Christmas, several big boxes arrived both at our house and the Swanson's. They all were from John and were marked, "Christmas." We opened our gifts Christmas morning as did Swansons. When the three of us (Chuck, David and I) got around to opening John's boxes, we were delighted. There we found Nehru jackets, sari's, baggy pants, and caftans. We were busy putting all of this on over our pajamas when the phone rang. It was the Swansons. All six of them were dressing in John's garb, and I could hear gales of laughter. "Come on over," they said. I said we weren't dressed, and had our Indian stuff on over our PJs. "Well then, just put on your coats and boots over everything and come through the hedge." We did just that. The younger girls tried on everything—as did Bayliss and Chuck. It was one of the most fun times I have ever had.

We stayed for coffee and rolls, then trudged back through the hedge wearing our PJs, coats, and boots. No matter how much it snowed in Minnesota, the hedge path stayed open. That Christmas started it. From then on, we did this every year at one house or the other—coats over PJs and boots. If the neighbors noticed, they never said anything.

However, there was one thing they did notice. A couple of years later when the boys were all home from college, I detected an increase in traffic on our little dead-end street. I finally looked out, and there, bigger than life, was a very large snow lady with huge boobs. The boobs came complete with Maraschino cherries. This lovely creature adorned the front yard of the house of the president of St. Cloud State University—our house. I kind of liked her. She had a cute hat! Chuck and Bayliss weren't amused. The lady was vanquished with several whacks of a broom.

Bayliss and Margery were wonderful neighbors. One night when we were out of town, Bayliss very ably helped David rid our house of unwanted teenagers. It seems that word got out we were gone, and the rough crowd began to arrive. David was concerned and called Bayliss to come over. That was the kind of trust we all had with each other.

Over the years we were neighbors, we spent many long nights waiting for our kids to come home. We suffered through several minor car accidents, and, of course, had to endure several on-and-off romances. Jim and Margret's romance did not last, but they have remained good friends. We felt real sadness when Jerry Weyrens was killed in Phoenix while walking across the street. Each Swanson lost a parent during that time. But, I wouldn't trade those years for anything. What I miss the most about my house in St. Cloud is that lilac hedge and our wonderful neighbors.

We had only been in our home two days when we received word that Chuck's Aunt Marjorie Powell had died on the farm in Illinois. Chuck's family broke the prairie in LaSalle County near Tonica, Illinois, in 1856. By 1870 his great-grandfather Andrew Powell, along with his sons, established a farm of 640 acres, which was passed down through the generations. This land is flat prairie with some of the best crop-growing soil in the world. Through the years, the farms have produced a variety of crops and livestock, but today are primarily devoted to corn and soy beans. My work in the Agronomy Department while at the University of Illinois gave me some acquaintance with Illinois agriculture even before I met Chuck, and this has been invaluable to me in understanding our farm operation.

Chuck was an only child. His maiden aunt and bachelor uncle, Chester Powell, divided their land between Chuck and his two cousins. Chuck received the house and contents. We left immediately for the funeral. The next year, we spent a considerable amount of time cleaning out the house—after almost 120 years of family occupancy. We brought many lovely old pieces of furniture, glassware, and dishes to St. Cloud.

The first piece of business for us in St. Cloud was Chuck's inauguration. It was scheduled for March 4, 1972. Being from Duluth, I knew about March weather in Minnesota and couldn't believe they would pick that time. But March it was. I worked with the various committees and enjoyed getting to know everybody. It was a lovely affair and very efficiently planned.

My biggest effort was getting the boys to look decent. I gave up on hair cuts—just asked that their hair be neatly combed. But, I did want them to wear their suit coats for a family picture and the inauguration ceremony itself. They resisted. I said, "Look, this is your dad's big day. Please don't disappoint and embarrass him. He is so proud of you!" They complied. Today they laugh at themselves in the picture with hair down to their shoulders.

On Friday, March 3, Doc Severenson and his band played at an inaugural concert in Hallenbeck Hall, our very large gym. Seven thousand people attended in spite of a big snow storm that dropped eight inches of new snow. Chuck's dad and his wife, Istalena, were there. She was a Southerner from Carl, Georgia, and she thought the weather was lethal! Several able bodied college students carried her over the snow banks into the various events. She was a tiny woman—barely five feet tall.

The Inauguration itself was Saturday noon, March 4. Our Minnesota governor, Wendell Anderson, came and spoke as well as other Minnesota elders. I was proud of Chuck as he marched in behind faculty, students, and dignitaries. That evening we had a grand all-community dinner followed by the Inaugural Ball. We felt feted. After the Blood letter and other events of the sixties it was most reassuring to me.

Although returning to Minnesota sounded like the right thing to do, I knew from our Whitewater experience that, burdened with the responsibilities of a college presidency, we would need a retreat—a place to let down and restore ourselves. As it turned out, we found just the right place to relax, renew, and write our speeches, workshop materials, proposals, and anything else that needed inspiration. We also had just plain fun there. We still do.

We first saw North Eden on May 4, 1972. We had encircled St. Cloud with a two-hour driving radius and started to explore the lake country. We headed north in Minnesota but didn't have much luck. However, Chuck and I had vacationed several times in Northwestern Wisconsin and so we gravitated to that area. The lakes are small, sandy, clean and nice for kids. Most of them are surrounded by pine and oak woodlands.

On that day in May, our realtor drove us down a sandy, tree-lined driveway and there before us was a storybook log cabin facing Deer Lake. It was and is perfect, It seemed unreal—built from pines harvested on the property and designed by a Danish man like a cabin he had seen and loved in Norway.

It was small, but we didn't care. It had a sleeping loft and a hide-a-bed in the living room, plus a small walk-through kitchen and a full bath. A large fieldstone fireplace covered most of the Western wall.

Above: Dr. Charles J. Graham, president of St. Cloud State University, 1971 to 1981. Right: Chuck and Bonnie at the Inaugural Ball, St. Cloud State College, 1972.

Chuck and Bonnie at the Inauguration.

Dressing for the snow—Inaugural Ball.

The cabin at Deer Lake near Webb Lake, Wisconsin.

Across the front of the cabin was a screened-in porch facing the lake. The property included 400 feet of lake front and twenty acres. The problem was we couldn't afford it. We offered and counter-offered all summer. In the fall, we finally capitulated and paid the asking price. It became ours on November 1, 1972. It certainly was a bargain when viewed today.

This purchase was one of the best things we have ever done. Over the years, we have enlarged the cabin, preserving the original structure. Our three sons, their wives, plus ten grandchildren have grown up there in the summers. We pound nails and argue politics, pick blueberries, disagree over the size of the fish caught, and discuss teenage predicaments. Many times we just sit on the porch and reminisce. I've heard an expression for this interaction. It is sometimes called *family glue* and it describes us perfectly.

In the years at St. Cloud and Hamline, we would often have to spend fall weekends on the campus. That made for weeks without a break. So, we drove up Saturday night or Sunday morning and spent twenty-four hours "chilling" as the grandkids say.

We named our cabin North Eden because our farm in Illinois is in Eden Township and thus called Eden Farm.

That fall of 1972, I took my first class at St. Cloud toward my degree. It was called "Technology and Man." I doubt if anyone in the class knew I was the president's wife except the professor, and he didn't care. But winter quarter of 1973, I enrolled in the "Theory of Vocational Counseling" course that had just been required by law for persons with a Master of Science in Vocational Counseling.

I found myself in the class with a woman about my age who was on the Board of Trustees of the State College system. The instructor recognized both of us, and I think he thought we were spies. He called us up after class and said he couldn't have us in class. It made him too nervous. We said that we would remain in the background and do the work so well that there wouldn't be any question about our grade. He said he needed to talk to the dean. We prevailed, and quietly got through the quarter. In retrospect, I wonder why we didn't just offer to read the book, take the tests, and not come to class. My trustee friend in the class was the mother of almost grown children. She was trying to finish her degree and get certification.

My third experience was powerful. It was a practicum where I was assigned to do career counseling and job-seeking skills training at the St. Cloud Reformatory. This institution is a maximum security facility for young men, eighteen to twenty-three, who are

Bonnie graduates with an MS degree from the University of Wisconsin-Whitewater, 1973.

in major trouble with the law. I worked in the pre-release center with those who would be leaving soon and needed to learn how to get and hold a job. In fact, they had to have a job before they could leave the Reformatory.

My fellow young counselors said I would never get along there unless I learned to talk their language—the language of the streets. The boys were the same age as our sons, and I thought, "Wouldn't I look ridiculous acting and talking like them?" I felt like all of us made progress, but I also thought that many of them would be back. They just didn't have enough support on the outside—no stable base. Those who had sponsors, a caring parent, or grandparents, seemed more likely to succeed. This was proven by the Reformatory's statistics.

To get to the actual center, we had to go through four sets of heavy locked doors. My reaction to the outside doors was not unusual. Many people lock their front and back doors. We walked down a bare corridor and came upon a second set of doors. Once again, we had to present our ID before the guards would let us in. The guards seemed big and burly to me. This was the area that contained the inmates' cells. The doors clanked behind us, and now I was beginning to feel trapped. The third set of doors led to the educational wing of the prison, and those doors, too, clanked as we went through. Finally, we went through a fourth set of doors into the Pre-Release Center. When those last doors shut, my situation felt so final. I had to stay in until someone let me out! I couldn't imagine living under these conditions. I will never forget this experience and the sorrow I felt for the young men inside.

After this internship, I spent the summer of 1973 reviewing my six years of work, and then I took my comprehensive exams in July. I graduated from the University of Wisconsin-Whitewater with a Master of Science in Vocational Counseling in August, 1973.

At St. Cloud Chuck worked closely with Sister Emmanuel Renner of the College of St. Benedict and with Father Michael Blecker of St. John's. In talking to Sister Emmanuel, he mentioned that I had completed my masters in Vocational Counseling and was interested in career planning for women. She called me soon after that and said she had a problem. Would I meet with her?

The College of St. Benedict was established and geared toward young undergraduate women. She was starting to have older women coming in who wanted to return to school. Many had no idea what they needed or wanted. She asked, "Would you be willing to teach a course in career development for women?"

I agreed. I had never taken such a course or taught one, but I figured with my training and experiences, I could put one together.

St. Cloud is located in the center of Minnesota. It is the county seat of Stearns County and abuts both Benton and Sherburne counties. The area was settled by many German Catholics. A characteristic of the area is that many of the small towns have only a Catholic church. The churches are quite large and very beautiful. Most of the people in these towns are fun loving and outgoing. They invented the polka mass. But these same folks also were conventional and often paternalistic. It was under these conditions that I began my counseling of women. Sometimes, in my teaching and counseling, I ran into trouble.

Several years after my St. Ben's experience, I began teaching the same course at St. Cloud State through the Extension Service. My first class at St. Cloud went well. The women were enthusiastic and excited. Three days later, I got a call from one of the students—a woman about thirty-five years-old who told me that her husband had burned her books and ordered her not to return to the class. He didn't want a "book learnin" wife. At first, she was too afraid to meet with me, but finally, we were able to have a coffee together. She never came back to class. She said that she needed her husband. I told her if she ever wanted help, she knew where I was.

The next event happened in much the same way. The woman did not show up for class the second week. She called and asked to meet me. Her husband also objected to her taking the class. She told him she wanted to take accounting and writing courses to be able to help him with his family business. He eventually "let her come" on the promise that she would tell no one what she was doing. She wanted to make certain I would not give out her name. I explained that, as a counselor, I could never divulge the name of a client or participant. Her husband told her that no one in town must ever hear about her going to school. It was close to a threat. Both women were from small rural towns in Central Minnesota near St. Cloud.

In the early 1970s, the Vietnam War dragged on. Our students were restless, but we had no open demonstrations until the bombing of Cambodia. The anti-war student leaders at St. Cloud, St. John's, and St. Ben's decided to stage a rally. Chuck heard a rumor about this and was trying to get prepared for anything when several of the organizers came to him and explained just what they would be doing. They planned to march to Lake George located in a small park near downtown St. Cloud. There they would express their concerns with teach-ins, speeches, and other forms of voicing opposition to the war.

Before they left, they took down the American flag that was hanging in front of the administration building. Not wanting any more incidents, Chuck and his vice-president waited until the students left for the rally and put it back up.

What happened at the rally was amazing and wonderful. Some of the sociology professors at the colleges asked their students to size up the crowd—students, professors, business leaders, young and old. They were to submit a paper about this aspect of the rally. Another group of psychology professors asked their students to look at and report on the actions and emotions of the crowd—crowd psychology. And the city of St. Cloud set up a voter registration booth at the park. The demonstration was peaceful. It was a truly inspiring event.

At about the same time in 1974, when I was forty-four, I had a personal experience that gave me pause. When I sought to have a tubal ligation for birth control, my doctor said he could do it but not at the St. Cloud Hospital. The hospital was a regional hospital, large and modern, but it was run by the Catholic diocese. They would not permit any birth control procedures to be done there. My doctor referred me to Methodist Hospital in the Twin Cities. The hospital put on my record that I had undergone a D and C, but I knew the doctor had done what I requested. The procedure is called "band-aid" surgery and the band-aid was in place. When I next saw my St. Cloud doctor he said, "You wouldn't want anyone in St. Cloud to know about this. We're protecting you!"

I had thought long and hard about having this done. Our boys were twenty-two, nineteen, and fifteen. I had finished my degree and started on my career. We didn't think it was the time for another child. It never occurred to me that anyone in the community would know and more importantly, would care!

In 1959 we first had a foreign student living in our home when Zeynep Man from Istanbul, Turkey, joined us. She was admitted to River Falls State College and helped me with the boys in exchange for her room. She spoke English very well. The first thing she did was to pin a "God's Eye" on David to ward off the "evil eye." I still have the pin. It is quite a small stone with a hole for the pin and an eye in the middle of it. David was six months old at the time.

We learned a lot about Muslim culture from Zeynep. One day she announced that a mother of three boys would be greatly honored in her country. There I would live "like a queen in a hut instead of a slave in a palace." The palace was our home. She thought I worked entirely too hard. When I asked her how a mother of sons got help, she said there was always a poor relative from the country who would come to live with them and help the family.

In the fall of 1969, Amir Firouzabadi arrived on our doorstep from Teheran, Iran. He was seventeen, John's age, and lived with us for a year. Amir also spoke English quite well. He and John were seniors at Whitewater High School in Wisconsin. Amir taught me a few more Muslim and Middle Eastern concepts.

To Amir, it was a man's world, and whenever I gave him a direction such as, "Be home at 6:30 for dinner," it didn't seem to compute.

Amir with Bonnie and Chuck Graham.

Finally, when I asked Chuck to speak to him. He would say, "Yes, sir," and respond immediately.

In later years, Amir said, "How did you ever put up with me?" I said it wasn't easy. Amir was the youngest of four sons. He said his mother was revered for having produced four boys and she, too, had help from relatives.

In 1971, to get the overseas programs started in St. Cloud, Chuck hired a very able director, Robert Frost. Soon, we had students studying in Alnwick, England; at the Duke of Northumberland's Castle; in Denmark, Spain, and Germany. Other countries in South America followed. We began having more and more students from overseas coming to our campus. It made for a rich life.

From time to time the mayors of the various foreign cities came to visit. We would entertain dignitaries at our home from both St. Cloud and our overseas locations. Many student delegates came also. One Christmas, we had a carol sing with the Danish students. I thought what they were singing sounded like a drinking song, It was rollicking, and had many verses. They confessed to me upon leaving that it was. They figured that we wouldn't know the difference.

Jim, David, and I enjoyed visiting overseas sites with Chuck. Today, St. Cloud State University has 900 foreign students on campus and 400 American students studying abroad. In 1973, the Grahams had their own overseas program. John went to southern India for a year as a student from the University of Wisconsin-Madison, and James was an AFS student in Brazil.

The year 1975 was a big one for the women of St. Cloud. The United Nations pronounced that year as International Women's Year, and we celebrated with our own Women's Conference March 20-22. The event was sponsored by many diverse women's groups in St. Cloud such as the American Association of University Women and the League of Women Voters. I was pleased to be asked to be presenter. I felt I could act in my own capacity and also represent the College. My topic was "Women Re-entering the Job Market."

At that time, we had a small group of militant feminists on campus. They had a "women's house" in town. The group seemed quite radical to me—even anti-men. I loved my all male family. I felt compassion for them as they tried to negotiate the new rules. John said if he opened a door for a woman, he was called chauvinistic; if he didn't, he was a clod! He felt he couldn't win. I knew then—and know today—that we have to work together, men and women, and that war with men won't work. In the election of 2008, we put seventy-seven female members in the House of Representatives and eighteen in the U.S. Senate. We expect and hope the men in Congress will work with their female counterparts for the common good.

In 1975 I was asked by a friend from Reading Room, my book club, if I would like to help out with the St. Cloud United Way. They needed someone to help organize the Professional Division, to work with the lawyers. I was to coordinate their efforts. My first meeting was with a young lawyer in town. I arranged to have breakfast with him at Perkins, a popular family restaurant.

When I told my mild-mannered husband, he rose up and said, "You can't do that—have breakfast with just the two of you in a public place? It just isn't right!" I was flabbergasted! Chuck said it wasn't right for a married woman to be seen in a public place with a man—never mind that he was also married. I said that we are just going to plan the lawyer's approach to their campaign for the United Way. We discussed the issue some more and, finally, I agreed that we would sit in the middle of the restaurant, totally exposed. No hush, hush rendezvous. I told Lee the story when he arrived and he laughed, but made sure that everyone we knew who came in was told we were about United Way business. After that, I regularly met with both men and women without discussion or repercussions.

In 1978, I was asked to head the Professional Division. In that position, I was now on the United Way Board. It was a very successful organization. We always met our goals. Folks seemed to work well together. But, since St. Cloud was growing, and new ideas, religions, and mores were taking hold, we had to make some difficult decisions. The three agencies most affected were Planned Parenthood, Lutheran Social Service, and Catholic Charities. There was opposition to Planned Parenthood because it gave out birth control information and educational materials. I knew how most people felt about abortion, so I pled with them simply to help Planned Parenthood with their prevention efforts. My efforts were to no avail. We didn't fund Planned Parenthood.

Next came the problem at Lutheran Social Service. Someone on the board heard that if you called LSS, they might refer you to the Minneapolis LSS, and "those people" might give you an abortion referral. None of this could be proved, but it was enough for the United Way and the community. The majority of the board decided not to fund Lutheran Social Service. That left us funding only Catholic Charities in a community that was over fifty percent Protestant by then. I said, "It won't work—Funding will go down. We serve the whole community as a United Way." That is exactly what happened. The next year, Lutheran Social Services was funded. In 1979 I was made the first woman president of the St. Cloud United Way and really enjoyed that role. I made life-long friends there.

Along with all of these activities, I was asked to be on the Great River Regional Library Board. At that time, they were about to build a new Central Regional Library in St. Cloud. The argument went on and on as to where to put it. Most of the board wanted a central location—downtown and near a bus line. Many citizens wanted it out further—near a park and easier to drive to. However, you would need a car to get there. I gave speeches around town about the pros and cons of the library and the site.

In the meantime, Chuck was embroiled in a controversy regarding a bridge over the Mississippi River and the connecting road that went through the campus. The newspapers would print "Graham said" but not indicate which Graham. We asked them to use our first names. Chuck did not want to be responsible for my problems and controversies, nor I his.

I worried about how these issues, including my working in St. Cloud, would affect him and the university. We talked about it from time to time. I got a clue from him early on in his presidency when a business man from town asked him, rather snidely, "How does it feel, Dr. Graham, now that your wife is working?" I was at one end of the dinner table and Chuck at the other. I cocked my head to hear his answer. With his usual broad smile, Chuck said, "I worked to support her the first twenty-five years of our marriage and I'm counting on her to support me the second twenty-five." End of discussion.

As president of a St. Cloud State College (it was changed to university in 1975) Chuck attended the annual meetings of the Association of State Colleges and Universities. The presidents met to discuss common problems, trends in education, and recent federal and state legislation involving education. They met at very interesting locations throughout the U.S., such as Boston, New Orleans, and San Francisco, always on the off-season—November. Air fares and hotel rates were cheaper that time of year. Also, all campuses had a Thanksgiving vacation and the presidents could most often get away then. I went with Chuck when I could, but I had to pay my own way.

The first few years' programs were planned with wives in mind. These were mainly sight-seeing activities. By the late seventies, the name for these events was changed from "wives" to "spouses." Spouse was used because we now had women presidents, and their husbands or significant others often came. We wives or spouses still had some tours, but we were encouraged to attend our husband/wife's sessions. I found some of these very interesting! As part of the spouse's program, a series of sessions was introduced on the "The Role of the President's Spouse"—mostly wives in this case. What a hornet's nest! The talks would go on and on. Every spouse had a different opinion of his or her role. Mostly the wives took part in the discussion. Some wanted to be paid for their efforts. Others were "joined at the hip" to their husbands and his job and even got daily directions from the president's office. They considered themselves a team, and they wouldn't consider being paid.

There were many in the middle who felt like I did. I did not want to be tied down to a contract. I enjoyed the freedom and the juggling. I didn't want to give up all the entertaining we did, nor would I give up my counseling and volunteer activities in the community. I felt that I could flexibly contribute to both town and gown. Today the issue is still hot. Recently, a friend of mine, whose husband is a new college president, signed a contract for $1,000 a month to carry out the duties of the president's wife.

However, not all of my or our activities were controversial. We had and still have many friends in St. Cloud. Our Highbanks neighbors were from all walks of life—golf course owner as well as a farmer, owners of the local radio station, a car dealership, and the Coldspring Brewery. With these friends, we rarely discussed education and its problems—a nice change for us.

We spent hundreds of hours at our boys' ball games and other sports activities. I continued to swim laps regularly. Swimming was and is my personal physical and psychological therapy. I had two social groups I especially enjoyed—a bridge foursome and an exercise club.

The bridge group met twice a month. We had a potluck salad lunch at one of our homes and then played bridge until 3:30 when school was out. The group consisted of Sue, the mother of one of David's basketball teammates whose husband owned an Insurance Agency; Marcia, whose husband was a doctor; Phyllis, a faculty wife; and me. As time went on, we got better and better acquainted and did more talking and eating and less bridge playing.

The end of the bridge games came when Phyllis and Marcia, who shared the same cleaning lady, found clothes missing from their storage closets. We suspected the cleaning lady took them but couldn't prove it. We laid out a large plan to trap her with possession of goods, but it didn't work. The police weren't interested because we couldn't prove anything. One day, Marcia and Phil found their belongings for sale at a local consignment shop. They asked for the clothes, and the owner said they belonged to her or the consigner.

In the end, the police got involved and caught the cleaning lady, but it was over a year before my friends got their clothing back. The court needed the items for evidence. My friends ended up feeling like the victims. We never played bridge again—just ate and visited.

The exercise club was a group of faculty wives. They met for an hour of exercise at 11:00 A.M. and then went to lunch. I was pleased to be invited to join. Gradually, the women gave up exercising (sore arm, sore leg, sore back) and just ate lunch together. Chuck teased me about my bridge club that didn't play bridge and my exercise club that didn't exercise. I thought it was unique!

One university group that was important to me was the International Wives division of the Faculty Women's Club. We met with women from all over the world who had come to St. Cloud with their faculty or student husbands. The aim was to help them acclimate: answer questions about grocery shopping, how to find a doctor or dentist, or even what to wear. We told them our conversations were confidential and no questions were considered silly.

One day the phone rang. It was one of the women in the group. She said she had a question that she was embarrassed to ask at a meeting. The question was, "Mrs. Graham, what is scratch?"

"Scratch," I said. "What do you mean?"

Her reply was that so often when someone brought something to the meeting that was good to eat, the contributor would say, "I made it from scratch." My foreign friend said she had searched all over the grocery store for scratch, but couldn't find it.

I was taken back and smiling to myself at my end of the phone line when I told her it was an American idiom meaning it was made from a combination of ingredients such as flour and sugar and did not come from a box! Her reply was, "I'm sure glad I didn't ask the question at the meeting!" Years later I had some of the same experiences in Japan!

I really enjoyed my book club called "Reading Room." The group was about as old as St. Cloud itself. It started in the 1880s because the newly arrived women residents needed books to read. They searched around until they found a room to rent in downtown St. Cloud, pooled their books, and started a small reading room, a precursor of the St. Cloud Public library. Each year our dues paid for special reference books for the library. Many of the members of the club were from "Old St. Cloud" families—very interesting and very nice. I learned a lot from them. A member of the club gave a book review each month. I think I was asked because the president's wife traditionally belonged.

In my last years at St. Cloud, I unknowingly became a mentor for several young women. When I was a student at the University of Illinois, I belonged to Phi Chi Theta, a woman's honorary professional business fraternity. In the late 1970s, that group organized at St. Cloud State. They heard about my affiliation and from time to time asked me to join them. I enjoyed my experience with the students. Years later I've met some of them and love to hear of their experiences in the world of work and home.

Our sons thrived and moved on in the 1970s. After John's year in India, he returned to the University of Wisconsin/Madison where he graduated in 1974. The years 1975 and 1976 he spent in the Peace Corp in the Congo teaching English as a second language in a French and Swahili speaking school. From there he attended the School for Advanced International Study at Johns Hopkins University in Washington, D.C. He received his master's degree in 1978. John married Martha Morris in 1979, and they moved to New York City where John worked for Salomon Brothers and Martha for Chemical Bank. They moved to London in 1982. Both were transferred by their employers. They have lived there ever since.

Jim returned from Brazil and graduated from high school in 1974. He attended Carleton College in Northfield, Minnesota, and graduated in 1978. David started college in 1977 graduating from St. Olaf College, also in Northfield, Minnesota, in 1981. He spent his junior year abroad at St. Andrews University, St. Andrews, Scotland, studying religion and political science.

My biggest satisfaction from being able to work (albeit part time) was helping pay the boy's college expenses. Jim went on to receive a DVM (Veterinary Science degree) from the University of Minnesota and David a law degree from Hamline University in St. Paul, Minnesota.

With the boys gone, we were excited about another opportunity that arose in the fall of 1979 to return to Washington, D.C. Chuck was asked to take part in an executive exchange between administrators in the government and administrators in higher education. The term would be from January through March 1980. Chuck was posted to the Department of Health Education and Welfare (soon to be the Department of Education) to work on the Higher Education Financial Bill.

We drove to D.C. through an Ohio snowstorm and arrived safely. Our apartment was provided by the program. It was on Pennsylvania Avenue near George Washington University and only a few blocks from the Kennedy Center and the Watergate complex! Watergate included a rather large grocery store, very handy for me. I could walk to the Smithsonian and the National Gallery of Art. It was a perfect place to spend three months.

It was exciting and rewarding to renew our friendships from our former stints in D.C. We were able to visit with Senator Proxmire and his wife, Ellen, and Les Aspin, Chuck's intern under Proxmire, who was now a Congressman from Wisconsin. We also renewed our friendship with my cousin Bill Carroll and his wife, Bunny, who still lived in Bethesda, Maryland, and our friends from our previous stays in Washington invited us to join them for dinners and hiking. The treat for me was that for three months I was able to visit the exhibits at the Smithsonian that we passed over when the boys were with us, such as the First Ladies' Inaugural Ball Gowns, White House China, and Oriental Art.

At the end of March, our friends Ruth and John Prentice from Whitewater, Wisconsin, came to visit us. They had never seen Jefferson's home, Monticello, near Charlottesville, Virginia. We headed out the next day and found ourselves in a snowstorm near Charlottesville. As Minnesotans, we didn't think the storm was so bad, but the Virginians did. They closed Monticello, and advised us not to leave town.

The Howard Johnson had one room left. It had two double beds. The hotel objected to two couples in a room, but we prevailed. What did they think we were up to? The next day was clear, beautiful and snowy. The University of Virginia campus was like a story book fairy land, but Jefferson's home was not open. No one came to work! We had to leave because of Ruth and John's airline tickets. We felt sorry for them. We had visited Monticello several years earlier.

Chuck felt his work in the Executive Branch of the government had been very rewarding. We returned to St.Cloud after the first of April. I resumed my United Way duties and other obligations. It was a nice break for us.

As the 1970s wore on, Chuck began to feel that ten years would be enough as president of St. Cloud State University. He had worked hard to improve the caliber of education at St. Cloud with emphasis on liberal arts and foreign programs. The Business College was accredited during his term. He believed strongly in faculty participatory governance with a faculty senate, but by 1977 the state universities had been unionized, and he did not like the adversarial positioning between faculty and administration. He looked forward to being a distinguished emeriti professor at St. Cloud and teaching political science full-time.

I thought this was a great idea. My career in employment/career counseling was taking off, and I knew town and gown folks from all walks of life. I liked living in St. Cloud.

∽ 6 ∽

The Eighties

Some New Beginnings

But our idyllic plans were not to be. The Methodist bishop had heard that Chuck might be retiring. He knew Chuck from the many times they had met at the Methodist Annual conference in St. Cloud. There he had heard Chuck talk on the value of liberal arts and the exploration of social and religious issues. The bishop asked Chuck to apply for the position of president of Hamline University, a private Methodist liberal arts college, in St. Paul, Minnesota.

Was this Divine Intervention or God's calling? We will never know. After much thought and talk, Chuck accepted. We moved to St. Paul the summer of 1981. At that time, the Hamline student body consisted of 1,200 undergraduate students, a Law School of 400 students, and a master's degree program in Liberal Studies.

Our home, which had been the president's home for years, was the big White House located in the center of campus. It was beautiful, and I loved it. Built in 1903, it was located on the north side of Hewitt Street across from Hamline. In 1947, the Hamline trustees moved it to its present site on campus. It was large and always painted white. Across

The White House at Hamline University, where we lived on campus.

the front of it was a lovely portico with big raised pillars on each side. I enjoyed being there. It was gracious living.

Upstairs were four bedrooms and two baths. A lovely small half-bath, nice for guests, was on the first floor. We had two living rooms with a fireplace at each end, and a large dining room with easy access to the kitchen and pantry. This house, too, had a back stairway which was once again perfect for our boys and student guests to come and go undetected. Our favorite room was the three-season porch. That is where the TV was located, and it was our place to relax. The students who lived with us often served tea to the group that gathered there to watch the 10:00 P.M. news.

As soon as Chuck accepted the presidency, the trustees told us the kitchen was old and inadequate for entertaining. I could see that, but was taken back when they asked me to redesign it. The idea scared me.

I had never even looked at a kitchen design book. I asked to work with a kitchen expert, and between us, we produced a kitchen that I thought was very workable.

I liked being close to all the campus activities. However, I never realized how lonesome I would be there. Our only non-student neighbors were the Methodist minister and his wife and family. They were lovely, but three blocks away. I used to say there was nowhere to borrow a cup of sugar quickly!

This is the first time in our educational wanderings that we dealt directly with a Board of Directors. At first, I was intimidated at the thought. These folks were movers and shakers in Minnesota. I was especially concerned when one of the wives told me that she bought gifts for her grandchildren at Tarjay. I thought, "She shops for her grandchildren at a French store! That's out of my league!" Later I found out she meant Target. She's a gracious, outgoing lady, and I still value her friendship.

The wife of the Board Chairman, Lois King, was also a most caring person. Both she and her husband, Bill King, were Hamline graduates from the 1930s. She kept asking me if I was okay—was I adjusting to Hamline? For six months I assured her that everything was fine. Then one day tears came to my eyes, and I confessed that although I really enjoyed Hamline, I missed my St. Cloud friends and teaching. She put her arms around me and was such a comfort.

I learned a lot that day. Here I was fifty-one years old and not coping very well. Maybe I had moved one too many times. I had always prided myself on being able to adjust. Now I felt like an old car that had been driven by eight to ten drivers. I was still running, but not up to par.

I also learned that a stiff upper lip doesn't always work because the conversation or atmosphere isn't real. My friend didn't gossip, but the folks around me seemed very caring after that, and I began to move forward. I knew I needed to find a job—not for the money but for a chance to use my talents.

Finding a job after age fifty is never an easy matter, and I had other restrictions. I felt that I could work sixty percent of the time at the most, and I thought I didn't want to drive too far everyday—say to the Western suburbs. I knew very few people in the Twin Cities in my field, so I began by informational interviewing. I called the agencies where I thought there might be a place for me and made arrangements to go there and speak to someone who could tell me about their operations. This worked fairly well. I met one woman who began to give me leads. Eventually, after four or five months, I got several interviews, but no job. It wasn't age as much as we just didn't fit. At this point I was getting more tied up in Hamline affairs and I gave up for a while. This happens to many job seekers—the slump! I also began teaching one class a week at Metropolitan State University in St. Paul.

One day near the end of July when I was at our lake cabin I picked up a Twin Cities paper and for the first time in several months looked at the want ads. There was the perfect job for me! An agency called Women in Transition wanted a part-time counselor. From the first minute of the interview it was "right," and I was hired. The big trade-off was that the agency was located in St. Louis Park, a western suburb of Minneapolis, and fifteen miles from Hamline in St. Paul. I became quite adept in finding the safest routes in the ice and snow of our Minnesota winters.

The agency worked with women of all ages and stages. I conducted Job Exploration and Self-assessment workshops as well as teaching actual job-seeking skills. Our clients needed lots of help. They were out of work for many reasons. Some had been laid off, some were fired, and others were recently divorced or suffered from abuse. Some just wanted to go to work to support their kids in college. There were many reasons for their situations.

After the Civil Rights Act of 1964, women, by law, were given more equal opportunities, but one result was less or no alimony for a woman on the theory she could work and do her share. This situation was especially hard on older women who had been home when their children were young and often lacked workplace skills.

In other cases, women couldn't get up the courage to ask for a promotion because they thought they weren't good enough. Some were too intimidated to even imagine asking for a raise. Others couldn't conceive of asking their employer for on-the-job training, and the list goes on and on. These situations are prevalent even today. Along with my activities at the Women in Transition work site, I did special workshops on back-to-work skills for women soon to be released from drug treatment centers. Those workshops were conducted at the centers located around the Twin Cities.

The people at Hamline seemed fine with my working. Most faculty wives worked outside the home, and married women in the workplace were becoming more common. Hamline set up a daycare center while we were there to accommodate faculty, staff, and student families with children.

Some Methodist women were concerned when I didn't show up at the state-wide School of Missions held on the Hamline campus every July. It was often held at the same time as our family reunion at the cabin. I saved the vacation date a year ahead as did John and his family who came from England to join Jim and David and their families. We only got together once a year, and it was important to all of us. I often welcomed the Methodist women before I headed north. I tried to show them that as a Methodist woman, myself, I cared.

When Chuck arrived at Hamline, money was tight. We had a unified budget, and I felt that if I asked for something new for the house, our students would be denied test tubes in the labs. One day, a piece of the front portico fell off the top of one of the columns that held up the front entryway to the house. That did it! We had to get the entrance fixed. The attic also became an emergency project when the squirrels got in and began chewing the electric wiring and, even worse, from my point of view, my stored Christmas decorations!

Chuck asked the maintenance crew for help with the squirrel problem. They gave us live traps to catch them. We did capture quite a few, and Chuck took them to Como Park two miles away and let them go. We were certain they got back to Hamline before we did. It became apparent that the attic also had to be repaired.

In the spring of 1982 after we had been living in the White House about six months, I decided it would be nice to plant a few flowers around the foundation. My dream was to have flowers six months of the year to brighten up our home and to place on the tables when entertaining.

My day had started out quite nicely. I'd arranged some time during the first week in May to buy plants. I am not a gardener, so relied on my minimal knowledge of what blooms when, and some good advice from the local nursery.

Friday dawned bright and clear, and since it was my day off, I figured this was the morning. With much difficulty and little know-how, I spaded up the hard earth, dug 100 holes, one for each little plant, patted down the soil and watered. I was a mess but so happy, and I finished in time to change my clothes and go to a luncheon.

That Friday was carnival day at Hamline. It was organized and sponsored by the students to raise money, most of it going for a new field track. In the afternoon my husband was volunteered to be the victim in the dunking tank: in other words, if someone was able to throw the ball and hit the circle, the mechanism was released, and Chuck was dunked in a vat of cold water.

I returned home from my luncheon about 2:30 P.M., and the first thing I did was to rush out to admire my new plants. Imagine my dismay and shock when I discovered that my entire garden had been rototilled! My little seedlings were scattered everywhere. Many were demolished. We had never lived in a manse before, and it hadn't occurred to me that our garden was under the jurisdiction of the yard crew. The young students simply did as they were told!

I dissolved. I was a very busy lady, working two-thirds time, carrying the role of the president's wife, and trying to find time for my children and grandchildren. This seemed like the last straw to me. I changed my clothes, and with tears running down my face, I got down on my hands and knees and rescued every little plant I could. It was about 3:45 P.M. when I finished. I was a muddy mess!

Just as I got back inside, my husband arrived home. He was very cold and very wet. I talked him into taking a hot shower and going upstairs to bed with a warm electric blanket. I still hadn't had a minute to clean myself up.

There I was, standing in the hallway covered with dirt and mud from head to toe, when the doorbell rang. The knees of my jeans were caked with mud as were the elbows of my shirt. Worst of all, my face was dirty, and my now dried-up tears had left muddy streaks running down my cheeks. I was startled!

Since the White House at Hamline was both the president's house and our home, we had a system regarding the doorbells. I knew from the sound of the bell that it was the side door used mostly by family and deliveries. In my misery, and without thinking, I opened the door. There stood our Methodist minister friend with one of the most handsome and distinguished Black African men I had ever seen. My friend said, "Bonnie, I want you to meet the bishop of Kenya." Then he said, "Is Chuck home?—I mean, President Graham, at home?"

I thought of my husband's situation—tucked in bed in his underwear—looked at my messy appearance, and gasped. My thoughts raced in six directions at one time—none of them very effective. Finally, I started to stammer about my flowers and Chuck in the dunking tank. The bishop looked blank. I am sure he thought he was in the wrong house.

I excused myself and went to get Chuck. I thought to myself, "This is a ludicrous situation!" I said, "Get up, dear. The bishop of Kenya is here!" He had trouble believing me. I didn't blame him. He appeared a few minutes later in his robe and slippers. I washed my face and went to prepare tea. Neither of us remembers the conversation. I just know the bishop didn't invite us to visit him should we ever get to Africa.

It was nice of our friend to bring the bishop around to meet us. I just wished he had called ahead. But this experience prepared me to not be surprised at anything!

I ask myself why this story calls to me so many years later. I'm convinced it's not just the humor of it. I think it's because the story so clearly illustrates my frustrations between being myself, the flowers destroyed, and the twenty-four-hour confusing demands of my role representing the university and the United Methodist Church.

The second year we were at Hamline, several faculty wives came to me and said they were organizing a group to raise money for scholarships for Hamline students. They called their organization Friends of Hamline. It also included trustee wives and Hamline women staff members. They had in mind an Art Auction. The art would come from local artists with a few pieces provided by a dealer from New York. I never realized how much work it would be.

We had to organize on three levels. The artists had to be contacted, and the art collected and displayed. Secondly, we had to plan the dinner and the physical aspects of the auction itself, and finally, we had to create an invitation list, design the invitations, and take reservations.

With a lot of cooperation, we got it all together and held an art auction for three years in a row raising about $10,000. I enjoyed using my organizational skills and working with the various Hamline constituents. I will always be grateful to the late Mike Price, a well-known Hamline sculptor and faculty member, for his devoted help.

Our Hamline house was a busy place. During our six years there, we had a stream of students living with us, including my niece, and two students from St. Cloud who were Jim's friends. These young people were all taking temporary courses or interning in the Twin Cities. David moved into the third floor in 1984 to attend Hamline Law School, and Jim joined us in 1986 while he attended the College of Veterinary Medicine at the University of Minnesota. Along with this crowd, we had our Boston terrier, Sir Hamline Piper. As I look back, we all coexisted quite well.

We did have a glitch now and then. Since we were cooking at different times, I had a kitchen rule. If you use the last of the ketchup or soy sauce or other such items, put it on the grocery list. It drove me crazy to come home from work tired and worn out, grab for something at the last minute, and find it not there. One day after hurrying home from work, I looked for the soy sauce to put the finishing touches on my wok cooking. It was gone. I had a soy sauce fit. It was funny and not funny, but the boys got the picture.

By inviting me to live with them and attend the University of Illinois, my Aunt Lenore and Uncle Ernest had provided me with an opportunity of a life time. There was no way I could repay them, but I knew I could pass on that opportunity. At St. Cloud and Hamline we had big houses. Along with the students who lived with us at Hamline, we had two of my nieces live in our home while attending St. Cloud State. Chuck, an only child, was always a good sport about our enlarged family.

Our second son, Jim, and Helen Cowell were married in June 1981 after Jim graduaed from Carleton College. They lived in Brainerd where Jim worked for Minnesota COACT. He was also taking science courses from Brainerd Junior College in preparation for veterinary school. Our oldest grandchild, Lindsay Kathleen Graham, was born March 16, 1984. She was adorable—a girl at last!

Soon after Lindsay's birth, Jim's family moved to St. Paul where he was enrolled in the College of Veterinary Medicine. Helen had two daughters by a previous marriage, Shirley, ten, and Kasey, five. They were part of our family, too. In reality I now had three daughters.

Jim and Helen were divorced in 1986. I had never dealt with divorce personally, and it was hard for me. My problem was I thought of Lindsay as the daughter we lost in 1964. When Helen took her back to Brainerd, it was like losing my girl all over again. One of my fellow counselors was very supportive. Gradually, I healed. Today my twenty-five-year-old granddaughter is a college graduate, and recently married to Kevin Bourgo. She is a great friend.

Our oldest grandson, Benjamin Morris Graham, was born to our son John and Martha in 1985. His brother, David Hughes Graham, followed in 1987. They were born in England and are dual citizens of the United Kingdom and the U.S.A.

Our third son, David Powell Graham, married Therese Marie Pautz on July 23, 1988.

At Hamline, Chuck continued to emphasize the importance of foreign studies and arranging exchanges that would bring students here from all over the world. One such exchange was with Peking University in Beijing, China.

The first student to come was Min Lu, a physical education major. Min spoke excellent English, which she had learned from the Voice of America. She said she hid her radio under her pillow every night so she could listen. Min's work-study assignment was to help me when we entertained at the White House, which was often. She was a great ambassador. She mixed well, answered questions about her homeland, and was easy to work with. The next year Feng Ming Liu arrived. He was studying law at Hamline Law School. Min was given the job of helping him get acquainted with our campus and customs. Before the year was out, they appeared at our door asking us how to get married in the United States.

We helped them with the necessary paperwork. Then Min and I got busy planning a wedding at the White House. It was the perfect place to have such an event. Chuck represented her family and proudly walked Min down our lovely long staircase. This was his chance to be a father to a daughter. Min looked beautiful. She wore a borrowed white wedding dress. It fit her tall, statuesque body perfectly. In her arms, she

The marriage at the White House of Min Lu and Feng Ming Liu, both exchange students at Hamline University from Beijing University, China. Chuck proudly escorting the bride down our central staircase. May 1985.

carried two dozen artificial red roses that she had purchased at K-Mart. She was very happy with them, and refused my offer for a real bouquet several times. Her jet-black hair and sparkling eyes completed her look. She and Chuck both smiled radiantly as they walked down the long staircase.

Our vice-president, Dr. Ken Janzen, an ordained minister, married them. Stephen Young, dean of the Law School, represented Feng's family and read their greetings. The Chinese students from the University of Minnesota provided food for the reception. It was authentic Chinese food, and delicious. A year later, just before they left Hamline, they had a baby boy, and we were Chinese grandparents.

Debbie Meier, Bloomington, Minnesota, and Min Lu, Beijing, China, helping serve at the White House.

As a result of the exchange, in 1984, Chuck and I and Dean Young were invited to visit China. At this time, China was a tight Communist country. The Cultural Revolution had just ended in 1980, and our two Political Science professor guides had been "sent down" from the university to a collective farm for most of that time. They were accused of being "rightists" because they could read, write and speak English. We spent a week with them touring China before arriving in Beijing where Chuck met with the president of Peking University and other officials.

I was looking forward to visiting Beijing because Min had arranged for us to meet her mother. However, the Communist neighborhood

124

governing work group, the Danwei, decided she shouldn't see us. Our professors were helpless—they could do nothing. They felt sorry for us, and I felt sad, too.

I was especially interested in the women of China. Many had assumed party responsibility during the revolution, but all the leaders I saw during those two weeks were men.

We had one women guide in Guilin. We discussed the "one child only" policy. She was a party member and was required to agree, but said it was hard on those in the countryside who needed the help children provided. She also admitted that many baby girls disappeared at birth. If a couple could only have one child, most Chinese wanted a boy. She had twin sons, and, of course, proudly kept both boys.

Throughout the years, I have been interested in the economy of China. As early as 1984 during our visit, we saw evidence of the beginning of capitalism and entrepreneurship.

When we were being driven to the Great Wall outside of Beijing, I caught sight of the magnificent structure from a distance. It was thrilling—my fifth-grade World History was before me. Imagine my surprise when we left the car and approached the wall. There stood a Chinese man with a camel. For a small fee, he offered to take our picture on his camel with the Great Wall as the background.

The Communist officials didn't seem to be concerned about him. Our guides said he could keep his money. We didn't have our picture taken, but we probably should have.

At other tourist stops, we were approached by women and children selling embroidered articles, wooden whistles, and other folk art objects. The children were so beautiful. I could barely resist them. But I couldn't bring home half of China!

During these same Hamline years, I was working hard counseling and teaching, and thoroughly enjoying both. I wrote and reworked much of the workshop material for Women in Transition, the agency where I was employed, and tried to keep abreast of the latest testing and self-assessment tools such as the Myers-Briggs and the MMPI inventories.

One of our biggest challenges was working our way through all the rules and regulations involving our clients. AFDC (Aid for Families with Dependent Children)—welfare—was the hardest to manage. We were governed by federal, state, and county legislation, but there was overlap. At times, it was confusing to all of us—counselors and clients alike. A case in point was Sally.

Sally arrived for our career counseling sessions in the fall of 1988. She was receiving AFDC or welfare payments. I noticed her immediately. She was an Afro-American woman, about forty-two to forty-five years old, neatly dressed, of stocky build with large brown penetrating eyes. She seemed at ease about being there. Our usual AFDC clients were eighteen to twenty-four years old, bewildered, dressed in blue jeans, and looking very uncomfortable. They were all sent to us by Hennepin County who paid for part of their counseling with us. At that time we already had a precursor to the Workfare program of today. We called it STRIDE. The women chosen for the STRIDE groups had their last child in school, thus freeing them, according to the county, to go to work and take on the responsibility of supporting a family.

At first Sally was reluctant to speak up in our group sessions, but gradually she began to tell her story. We were very grateful that she was willing to reveal as much as she did. Background stories helped the counselors assess skills, prior experience, education, and training possibilities for the participants.

Sally was raised on a cotton farm in Mississippi. She never knew her father. Her mother carried her on her back while she worked in the fields. She didn't give us any more details of her youth but said she ended up at the University of Wisconsin, graduating with a major in Physical Education.

In 1973, Sally had a son—no mention of his father. Soon after that, she came to the Twin Cities where she got a job as a transit inspector. Her task was to ride the buses all day and check on the driver. "Was he polite?" "Did he show any form of discrimination or abuse to her or others?" "Did he pocket the money?" (A common practice I was told). Some days she dressed like a professional working woman—other times like she was very poor. At times she was sent to other cities for a few days. Next door to Sally was a white family. The mother took care of Barry, Sally's son, while Sally worked. Barry lived with them during the days Sally was out of town. She told us it was a perfect arrangement.

In fifth and sixth grade, Barry began having academic trouble. By junior high, seventh grade, he was struggling. Sally was asked to come to the school many times. She complied, but found it difficult with her work schedule. Still, she made her appointments and tried to convince the teachers that she felt Barry had a learning disability. They didn't listen to her. Ultimately, the principal called her in and advised her to quit her job and devote full time to Barry and his problems. Sally resisted, but finally felt the pressure and resigned.

The first thing Sally did was to place Barry in a very highly rated private school. She fought for and received a scholarship for his tuition. Barry was tested and observed. It took some time, but the school was able to identify his problem, and Barry was on his way again. Meanwhile, Sally ran out of money. She said she had no choice but to apply for AFDC.

On the second day of our group, we talked about motivation. Sally, in a very solemn, mature way, took a letter out of her purse and began to read: "We note from our records that you have been on AFDC for three months and that you have a child in school. We require women in this situation to attend our Career Planning workshop and prepare to enter the job market in order to support yourself and your child."

Sally looked at us and said, "What do they expect of me?" Then she challenged the group, "What does society expect of us?"

I've spent years thinking about this. So many of the women I worked with came out of similar conflicting situations.

Sally stayed on with us and trained to be a group leader. She was very insightful. We all enjoyed her. Several years later, we were both working at a new agency. I was the manager/counselor and she a counselor/advisor. We were helping low-income working women keep their jobs and advance out of poverty.

In the middle of a staff meeting, I mentioned something about working poor women. Sally stopped me right there, and asked, "How can you speak for the poor?" She knew my husband was a college president at that time, but she did not know my background. I was stunned! I had made a point of not revealing myself except as a mother of teenage boys but decided this was the place to be frank.

I tell Sally and the group the same story I gave to the students in my "Marriage in the Family" class: How we had such difficult times in the thirties when my father couldn't work and how my mother, sisters, and I often assumed "male" roles. I also tell them that we had a vegetable garden, berries from the woods, boxes of food from our church, and clothes from our friends and neighbors. We all had second-hand ice-skates and one 1920s bike between us. There was no AFDC safety net. I watched my mother struggle; many times she could not pay the bills.

I told Sally this to help her understand that I was on her side. She replied, "I thought all Whites like you were rich."

I'd thought of Sally as my friend, but this was a real revelation. I began to feel comfortable enough to confess, "When I first saw you I wondered if you were here because your last child of a long string of children had just turned school age and you had been on AFDC all this time."

That opened the gate, and we began talking about stereotypes—how we operate on assumptions. I discovered that Blacks have as many stereotypes and misconceptions about Whites as we do about them. Our Native American counselor confirmed our observations and joined us in the discussion. It was one of the most revealing and heart-warming sessions of my counseling days.

After this meeting, we found ourselves looking for our "commonness." For starters, we were all women, most of us mothers of children, mostly teenagers. All of us were on our second or third careers. Some of us were married, and we all enjoyed our lunches out together. It was hard for me to retire and leave this wonderful group of colleagues.

Sally's son, Barry, was accepted into the University of Minnesota. He dropped out at the end of his sophomore year, telling his mother it was peer pressure. He didn't want to be a nerd. Sally told me, "I did the best I could."

In the 1980s, I was again involved in discussions about the role of the presidential spouses—this time at private college meetings. The rhetoric was much the same as that at the public university meetings. About the same time, I was asked to speak to the minister's spouses—mostly women—at the Minnesota Annual Conference of the United Methodist Church.

I told both gatherings the story of the boy who brought his report card home and told his father he was second in the class. His father was upset and asked, "Who was first?" The boy said, "It was a girl," to which the father retorted, "You were beaten out by a mere girl?" The boy looked up and said emphatically, "But, Dad, girls aren't as mere as they used to be."

I urged the women to speak up for themselves, to take a risk now and then. I felt, and still feel today, that a woman with a profession, career, or volunteer position in her own right can be a valuable asset in her role as spouse. Woman can see the community and its tensions from different points of view, thus they both gain insight. In this regard, I felt I was an asset to St. Cloud State University because I knew the community, especially the business leaders. When Chuck started the President's Club to raise money for the St. Cloud State University Foundation, I was well-acquainted with our contacts through my work in the United Way.

In one of the papers I wrote for the Private College Spouse's session, I noted that "president's wives know that the college president serves at the pleasure of the board, and sudden dismissals are not uncommon. The president himself might want out due to stress or poor health. The insecurity of the president's position is recognized by all. It is very real to the presidential couple. It seems to be a fact that a good, supportive, cooperative wife can be immensely helpful to her husband and to the college when things are going well, but she cannot save him when the danger signs become overwhelming. In view of this picture of the future, it would seem that a wife who is in partnership with her husband may become the most supportive of all if she becomes economically self-sufficient—if she pursues her interests and talents that lead to a career of her own or at least to the insurance that she is prepared for a career."

This philosophy may have been hard to take in the 1980s but it was reality.

The economics of the wife's situation was becoming more and more apparent. Spurred on by equal rights legislation in many states, the trend in divorce settlements was and is to make more equitable property settlements—each spouse getting half of the assets of the marriage—and requiring less alimony. This puts the presidential spouse and minister's wives in a very difficult economic position. Because she has spent or is spending her top earning years in a presidential home or parsonage, there may be no assets or a very small amount of assets to split. This is coupled with the fifty/fifty property split and the trend toward court settlements that assign alimony only temporarily until the wife can get retrained to support herself. Faced with this knowledge, a spouse cannot afford to be without a career—or at least must have a career option.

After I had given these talks and participated in many discussions about the role of the spouse, several people suggested I send copies of my speeches to the *Chronicle of Higher Education* and to the Methodist newspaper, *Concern*. This I did. I received a lengthy letter from Dr. David Riesman, author of *The Lonely Crowd* and a member of the editorial board of the *Chronicle*. By and large, he agreed with me. But he did say, "Perhaps on the basis of your own experience, you may somewhat underestimate the persistence of strong stag feelings in much of the population, including many business executives." This was borne out when my writings were not published, but my ideas were discussed in later articles, all written by men.

Another special international experience for Chuck and me and the Hamline community occurred on May 29, 1983. Madame Jehan Sadat came to our university to receive an honorary doctorate degree and to speak to us. I have always admired her. I knew of her works on behalf of Egyptian women. She started several women's cooperatives for rural women trying to support themselves and their families. Madame Sadat arranged for a supply of sewing machines to be donated to the women so they could make clothes cheaply and efficiently and sell the clothing items on the open market. She wanted Egyptian women to be freer. Although Muslim, she did not wear a veil. She felt Muslim fundamentalists were too restricting.

I also knew her as the wife of the president of Egypt, Anwar el-Sadat. I greatly admired Sadat for his peace efforts with Israel. Anwar el-Sadat was assassinated October 6, 1981. Madame Sadat's visit was less than two years later. Although she was still grieving, she was very gracious, easy to visit with, and very down to earth.

Jehan Sedat and Bonnie receiving guests at the White House, Hamlline University, May 1983.

131

We had a luncheon buffet reception for her at the White House. The guests included Hamline Board members, staff, and some city officials. She seemed to enjoy meeting everyone and made us all feel special.

After everyone had been through the line, we had about twenty minutes before going to the ceremony. The thought occurred to me that she might like to get away for a bit. I invited her to our rooms upstairs. She seemed grateful. She sat down on the big chair in our bedroom, looked around and spotted the pictures of our grandchildren. I told her their ages, and then asked about her little grandson who was with Anwar when he was shot. We continued to talk about her family and her invitation to teach in an American university in North Carolina. She was just finishing her doctorate. She, too, like all of us, was struggling with new roles, especially that of a widow with a family depending on her. Anwar was not wealthy. He was an army officer, and she could count on only a small military pension, if that. Jehan Sadat knew she would have to support the family.

In preparation for Madame Sadat's visit, we had groomed the campus, especially her walking path from the White House to the theatre where she would be honored. However, as we were leaving, the Secret Service was adamant that we take the back door route through the dumpsters, the potter's kilns and a parking lot. She didn't seem to mind. The day went well, and she wrote me a lovely thank you note.

A note: Jehan Sadat did receive her doctorate and is now a senior fellow at the University of Maryland. She is an example of an executive wife who spoke out and worked for what she thought was right for her community. However, she does admit in her book, *A Woman of Egypt*, that she angered the fundamentalists. I recognize that this is always a danger when a spouse takes a stand on a controversial issue. Communication between couples is essential, however, and Anwar supported her.

We left Hamline in June 1987. Chuck spent six years getting the budget under control and then felt it was time to go. He took a position with the Minnesota Private College Council and Fund as senior vice-president. We moved to our own home in Roseville, Minnesota, which is a short distance north of Hamline A private life at last—at least I thought so!

Our home at 1675 Ridgewood Lane was a story and a half, a blessing after all the stairs in the White House. We had two bedrooms and a bath upstairs, which was perfect for the grandchildren, and a bedroom, bath, den, living room, dining room, and kitchen on the main floor. The basement had a great recreation room and our study. Finally, the yard was pretty and the neighborhood friendly.

I continued to work at Women in Transition and took on more consulting jobs in such areas as Communication Skills in the Workplace, Long-Range Planning, and Goal Setting. Some of my former clients were now in administrative positions, and they asked me to come and present workshops for them. It was rewarding for me and very enjoyable.

As I might have expected by this time, after all the changes in my life, a call came to Chuck in the spring of 1988 asking him to take the position of interim president of Metropolitan State University in St. Paul, Minnesota, starting in the fall. Chuck accepted, and thus began fifteen months in a very happy situation for both of us.

Metro is a school without walls, but the main offices are located on the East Side of St. Paul in the old St. John's Hospital site. I had been teaching there since 1982, and Chuck was in on the conceptual discussions of the school in the early 1970s.

In 1988 Metro had been in operation for eighteen years The university was designed for upper level students—juniors and seniors. It especially appealed to men and women who had moved many times and had a disparate bunch of credits. We were able to evaluate their learning, accept the majority of the credits, and mold them into a plan that would lead to a degree. My women career counseling clients welcomed this chance to finally finish what they had started. Through many moves with their husbands, they often had to start over several times.

The course I taught was "Perspectives: Educational Philosophy and Planning." The description read in part: "This course is designed to help you explore your own lifelong educational needs and interests, some liberal educational philosophies and links between liberal learning and career preparation, the nature of learning in a multi-cultural and global society, and some current issues in higher education."

The Metro degree was a bachelor of arts in Liberal Arts. The founders felt that all students whether in computer science, business, nursing or traffic safety needed to live in their community and world. They should be able to understand their environment and what makes it work. I felt that way, too.

Many of my students came from local businesses. I often had workers from Northwest Airlines. One of my students was a pilot who flew for Mesabi Airlines. She was a petite Haitian woman—cocoa colored skin, dark hair and eyes, and always smartly dressed. One day she announced she would be missing the next class because she was going back to school to learn to fly a 747. Immediately, one of the men said in a loud incredulous voice, "You are going to fly a 747?"

She immediately replied with a quiet, calm, confident voice, "I am going to fly it, not carry it!"

Another class consisted of a Kuwaiti student, a Black African, a Native American, several students about twenty years old, and two older women about forty-five and sixty-five. At the time, Iraq had invaded Kuwait, and U.S. forces had landed there to liberate the country. My student was very worried about his family. I marvel at this modern world. He was able to talk to them daily on his cell phone. The class was very supportive of him and closely watched his country being freed. We cheered when he reported that his family was safe.

The Black African in the class revealed that he resented being called Afro-American as he was an Afro-African. He was from Ghana.

He said, "I am not American. Why use the label at all? Why not call all of us Black if you must?" The discussion was lively.

The older woman told of her great difficulties trying to get an education when she was young. We all learned from each other.

Metro was called a school without walls because at that time our classrooms were located in various sites all over St. Paul and the northern suburbs. I would get out my map, locate the building and drive there. I never objected until I was assigned a room in a junior high school with seats so small that none of us could sit down!

The 1980s ended for us with yet another big change in direction. In 1988, after Chuck had finished his term as interim president of Metropolitan State University, he was offered the position as assistant to the chancellor for International Programs with the assignment of starting a Japanese/American university in Northern Japan.

The story begins in 1978 when we visited a St. Cloud State University study program in Japan set up for St. Cloud artists by Laurie Hallberg. Laurie is a potter, and he arranged for his students to study at Mashiko, a town about 100 miles north of Tokyo which is a famous potting center. Our guide was Yutaka Morohoshi, a St. Cloud State faculty member and a Japanese citizen. He was home on a summer visit and met us in Tokyo. We all visited Mashiko together with Yutaka as translator.

Back in Tokyo, Yutaka announced he wanted us to meet his fiancé, Masako. Thus began a friendship for me of twenty-nine years. Masako was twenty-seven years old at the time. To me she looked like a beautiful Japanese porcelain doll. She was bright, well-educated, spoke English well and was fun to be with. Their arranged marriage was brokered by a "Miai" who met with his and her parents to bring the couple together. They dated several times before deciding to marry.

I was worried about Masako coming to St. Cloud, Minnesota. She seemed like a frail flower to me, and St. Cloud can be such a harsh place with its northern climate. Yutaka said he wasn't worried. I would help acclimate her. One of the first things I did was to introduce her to Laurie Hallberg because she was interested in art, and had always wanted to work in clay. By Christmas, Yutaka was complaining, "You made an American wife out of her: She doesn't come home in time to get my dinner!"

During the time she lived in St. Cloud, Masako completed a masters in English as Second Language (ESL). She works today, in 2009, part time in a high school and college in Japan. Her husband, Yutaka, is a college administrator and Japanese Television commentator.

My experience in Japan was very positive for me. I was ages eleven through fifteen during World War II, and the Japanese were the enemy. We met several Japanese citizens who apologized for starting the war, and it seemed to me we all felt badly it had happened. So when Chuck was asked to work with the Japanese on a new joint-venture university, I was quite pleased.

The idea of a university like Minnesota State University-Akita was first conceived by President Ronald Reagan and Premier Nakasone of Japan at a meeting in late 1987. This would be a means of handling our trade deficit with Japan. We would export education. Both countries needed English and Japanese leaders for business, scientific exchanges, and diplomacy, among other things. Under Governor Rudy Perpich, Minnesota made a bid for the school and was given the contract. The university buildings and grounds were owned and operated by the Japanese, but the faculty, staff and student activities were managed by the Minnesota State University System. The school is in Yuwa Town, a suburb of Akita city, located in northwestern Japan.

Chuck made many trips back and forth to Japan getting things started. I took vacation time and went with him several times. I helped when I could. We enjoyed watching the project grow, and looked forward to the opening of the university in 1990.

Although I was not prepared for many of my experiences in the 1980s, I survived and grew. Our days at Hamline, Metro State, and Japan were exciting, challenging and educational. In the 1980s we moved from a medium-sized public university to a small private college, to an inner-city institution and finally, to an international university in Japan. For the first time in my counseling career, I was working at an agency along with my self-employment as a consultant and teacher. During this time we had three grandchildren. Our life was full. By 1990 I was ready for our Japanese adventure and whatever would come next.

The Nineties

Life's Twists and Turns

The 1990s were ushered in for us with the opening of Minnesota State University-Akita in Japan. Yutaka Morohoshi became the first provost and thus Masako became his first lady. During trips to Akita, I spent a good bit of time with Masako. She was a faculty member teaching the Japanese language to American students. It was a hard spot for her to be both the provost's wife and a faculty member. However, the university needed her dual-language teaching expertise and Yutaka's dual-language administrative talents. They worked at keeping lines of communication open between themselves and other faculty members.

The Grand Opening ceremony was May 15, 1990. It was a political as well as an educational event with the Akita prefecture governor (who is like our state governor} and members of the Japanese Diet, the National legislature, included on the guest list. Since the university was operated by Americans under the American system, the men and their wives were invited to the grand opening dinner. At this point an uproar started. The Japanese men and particularly the governor let it be known

Bonnie dancing the Bon Odori with her Japanese women friends during the Fall Rice Festival, Yuma Town, Japan, fall 1993.

that women were not included in such events. Women did not often go out at night socially. They didn't attend public events, and it would change the whole atmosphere of the affair and spoil the fun. Moreover, the wives would need new, very expensive, kimonos. Yutaka retorted that we were going to handle this event the American way, and American wives would be attending. Japanese men were strongly urged to bring their wives. This was especially important because our lieutenant-governor, who represented the State of Minnesota, was a woman.

Then the Japanese governor, through his aides, sent word that the women wouldn't be comfortable there. Masako and I conferred. We agreed that the two of us, Chuck's secretary, and several Japanese women staff members who spoke both languages would circulate among the tables, talk with the women (sign language for me) and try to make them comfortable. I brought along pictures of my grandchildren and learned the Japanese name for grandson and granddaughter, also for son and daughter-in-law. I carried small hand-made American gifts in my purse

Chuck and Bonnie at the dedication of the Charles J. Graham Hall, Akita University, Yuma Town, Japan, 1973.

to give to the women guests while we conversed. These were Mug Rugs made by my mother. I received several lovely fans from them. It was a wonderful evening. The Japanese women looked beautiful. At the end of the evening, our new friends bowed and smiled and seemed very pleased.

We tried hard to avoid cultural confrontations. Our Japanese staff continually pointed out what we should or should not do in our daily lives. Yutaka used to say to us, "I don't want you embarrassing me." However, the societal expectations in Japan are very different from ours. Even though we did our best, we often erred. For instance, when entering a Japanese home or shrine, you always removed your shoes. Not to do so would defile the premises.

By 1993 the university was well established, and Chuck joined the Akita faculty as a professor of Political Science. He taught courses in American Government to the Japanese students who were in advanced English classes.

We left for Japan the first of September and stayed three and one-half months. Because we had been back and forth so many times, we felt at home immediately. Our apartment was near the campus. It was built for visiting professors. It was quite small and very Japanese except it had a western toilet, which meant sit versus squat. Our kitchen was tiny with barely enough room for a small table and a gas burner (no oven). The apartment had two bedrooms and a sitting room. One bedroom was equipped with tatami floor mats and futon pads for sleeping. The other was Western style. The sitting room contained a TV and two chairs. What intrigued us most was the pop machine out on the street in front of us. It operated all year because the winter was short and never extremely cold.

Every day in Japan was a new living experience. I was particularly interested in the roles of my Japanese women friends. One day a Japanese secretary at the university, who spoke English very well, invited me to a fourth grade picnic. I knew her little daughter and was pleased to go. It was a cultural experience I could never have imagined.

In the first place, when we arrived at the park, I saw no picnic tables. Of course, the Japanese sit on the ground on large mats which they brought with them. During the set up, the women and girls sat cross-legged around the mat and cut up the food for the *kiritampo*, chicken stew, while the boys played games with the gym teacher. Later all the children played and we had morning tea. Suddenly, there was a large chattering among the women. My friend said, "Would you like to know what they are saying?"

I said, "Yes, of course."

"They want to know about your red sweater. Do women your age (sixty-three) wear such bright colors in the U.S.?"

I learned quickly that older Japanese women do not. They wear only muted colors such as lovely mauves, grays, soft gray-blues and

Top: Thanksgiving 1993—Yutaka and Masako Morohoshi with Bonnie and Chuck. Bottom: Japanese friends at Minnesota State University-Akita—Left to right: Masako Morohoshi, Bonnie with arm around Tomayo Okomato, Yukiko Suda; back row: Chuck and Marcien Schroeder.

greens, but never red! Red is for the young and unmarried. On my next trip I left my red sweater at home.

During the afternoon break the topic turned to husbands. The question this time was, "Did my husband ever help with the dishes?"

I told him, "Yes, especially after a dinner party at night."

They were amazed. The women knew my husband was a professor. They said their husbands never went near the kitchen even if they asked.

In 1993 most Japanese women were "stay at home moms." At that time, Japanese working mothers were early pioneers. Daycare was almost non-existent although our university secretaries did manage to make arrangements for the care of their children.

Several times during that fall, Chuck and I were asked to join an English speaking group that met on Saturday mornings in Akita. The group was formed to help Japanese folks get together to practice their English. Their leader tried to have a few English speaking persons each week to stimulate the discussions and help the Japanese form words and thoughts. The participants were from all walks of life and both sexes.

I don't know how it began, but one day I found myself in what could have been an American family counseling session—Japanese style. In 1993, about twenty-four percent of the existing marriages in Japan were arranged. Whether arranged or not, a Japanese marriage is often described as "complementary." The husband and wife live in two different worlds that, together, complement or complete their living arrangement. In other words, the wife's world or "home" is the home, and she is solely responsible for the house, finances, and children. His world or "home" is his work where he spends all day, many evenings, and usually Saturday. His "home" also includes spending time after work and weekends with his business friends.

During this discussion, it became apparent to me and to the group present that there are many lonely people in Japan because of this separateness of men and women's worlds. One man confided that he was lonely because his wife scheduled her days and weekends with her women friends and her mother. When he did have time, she was not available. Several of the women in the group wanted their husbands to come to the discussion with them, but the men had work duties on this particular Saturday. Most were playing golf with business associates. In Japan, there are many places women cannot go alone. The Japanese women I met and interviewed wanted and needed male companionship.

While we were there, I saw gender roles played out in many different ways. Several times, we were invited to dinner in Japanese homes. In one family, both the husband and wife were over seventy years old. He was a physician and she was an excellent wood carver. He had been president of Akita University, and I felt the four of us would be on equal footing—so to speak. She cooked an excellent meal, but never sat down with us. She did join us later when I asked her, through her husband interpreter, to tell us about her carvings. We all had tea together.

The next dinner was in the home of a middle-aged electronics executive. He spoke excellent English and had traveled to the United States many times. When we arrived, we met his wife and teen-age children. However, while we ate the meal his wife had prepared, she remained in the kitchen and only came into the dining room to serve us. She did not seem unhappy about this. It seemed quite natural to them.

I do have an example of what I would call a progressive act on the part of the citizens of Honjo City—a community about thirty miles south of Akita. They were preparing to celebrate the twentieth anniversary of the opening of their Community Center and they asked me, a woman, to be their speaker.

I had written a paper for my Japanese friends called, "A Portrait of an American Family." They asked me to use it as the basis of my talk. In it I described both mothers and fathers participating in child rearing, work roles being exchanged, like Chuck helping with the dishes, and working wives in the United States. I used examples from our history to show how our society developed and why women had to become almost fiercely independent as they faced the hardships of settling a new land.

Then I went on to talk about common points for women and families in both countries. When I talked about women gaining a feeling of independence while working in the munitions and war effort factories, the older Japanese women, who had done the same thing, smiled and one even bowed. I gave this talk through an interpreter and it was fun to see the delayed reaction. I also mentioned how glad women in both countries are to have our "Three Sacred Treasures"—a Japanese term. These are a washing machine, a refrigerator and a TV. They all smiled, nodded and definitely understood.

Being the guest of honor at Honjo City was a high point for me. I was treated with much pomp and ceremony as the Japanese do so well. A delegation visited us several weeks ahead of time to officially invite me. They presented me with a lovely invitation tied with a blue ribbon. They invited Chuck to accompany me!

On the appointed day, we were met by the same delegates and driven to Honjo City. Honjo City is a medium-sized Japanese town about of about 30,000 people. The community center was in the middle of the town on a lovely old street. The building was rather plain looking on the outside as many Japanese buildings are, but with an open patio inside full of greenery. The meeting room was on the second floor.

However, before going there I was taken down the street to the home of the woman chairing the event so I might freshen up. There I stepped into true Japanese atmosphere. Her home looked like a store front from the outside but was beautiful inside. There were sliding doors everywhere. The furniture was simple and low with large old decorative vases sitting about. I was most impressed with the outdoor patio that brought the outside in when the sliding doors opened.

After the celebration, we were invited to dinner at the home of one of the committee members. Since there had been some drinking during the afternoon, we were met by a line of taxis to drive us to our next stop.

I remember many things about Japan, but one thing has remained indelibly in my mind: the safety of women was never doubted. I often walked alone a mile and one-half to the railroad station at Wada to take the train to Akita City. I started out through the forest, then on the paths through the rice paddies and finally through the small town to the station. Women alone are not attacked—or rarely attacked. Men take their sexual desires to "Love" hotels (designated by a large heart in front) or houses of prostitution. All women, whether young or old, are respected. We never locked our car or our apartment. When I returned home, I was angry at having to be so careful all the time.

After our stay in Akita, Chuck stayed on with the state university system and taught classes at Metro State and St. Cloud State universities. He retired in the spring of 1995, and I officially left our agency in 1994, although I continued to do consulting after that.

About this time, Chuck received a letter from our alma mater, the University of Illinois, notifying him that he was the recipient of that year's Liberal Arts and Science Alumni Achievement Award. It was a well-earned cap on his career. The presentation was at Homecoming in the fall of 1995. We were wined and dined and given an in-depth look at the new facilities on the campus. He felt honored. We both did.

In the summer of 1990, our Japanese adventures coincided with the arrival of my mother, Kathleen Eackle Ure, to live in the Twin Cities. She was eighty-four at the time.

My mother was living in Loveland, Colorado, near my brother and sister-in-law. They had been nursing both of her parents, and the responsibility was getting very hard for them. Mom was having health problems. I am twelve years older than my brother and the oldest child in my family, so it was my turn to pitch in and help.

My sister and I had been back and forth many times to see mom through several surgeries. I knew I could not take care of her from a distance. That summer, I persuaded her to move to St. Paul to be near us. We found an apartment for her in a senior hi-rise not far from our home. It provided many services such as a hot meal at noon, a bus to the grocery store, and various types of entertainment. She had never learned to drive, so she was dependent on me to help her get around.

Mom had contracted polio as a child of two, and her left leg and thigh were beginning to weaken again with Post-Polio Syndrome. She used a cane and a walker, but as the nineties wore on, she had trouble with falling.

I visited her several times a week—and every day as the years went by. I also took her shopping and to the doctor, On nice days we went on sight-seeing excursions in the car. We included her in all of our family activities. Her mind was our family encyclopedia, and she remembered all of our names, dates, and circumstances. She loved reading and writing poetry, and she chronicled the Ure family doings in lively and often very humorous poems. We have a copy of this family treasure.

Kathleen E. Ure on her ninetieth birthday, August 1996.

I enjoyed my mother's senior friends immensely. For all of their troubles, aches and pains, they often had great senses of humor. One day I was helping them fill out the forms for a flu shot. On the form where it said, "Are you pregnant?" they all agreed to say "Yes." The trouble was that the nurse attendant, a man, didn't think it was funny. They were disappointed.

On mom's ninetieth birthday in 1996, we had a big party for our whole family and the residents. Her grandchildren put on a program. There was tap dancing, ballet dancing, a karate exhibition, two piano pieces, and a group sing-along. Our family from England came. My sisters and brother and their children and grand-children all participated. It was joyous.

I enjoyed those years with my mother, but I realized my role as a woman had again changed. Now I was the sandwich generation, since we'd had four more grandchildren born during the 1990s. I found it hard to move in so many different directions at once.

Our new grandchildren were Matthew Kelly Graham, born in London, England, October 23, 1992, to Martha and John Graham. He joined his brothers Benjamin and David. Our son, David Graham, and Therese Pautz had two boys born in the 1990s, Andrew Charles Pautz Graham on June 8, 1993, and Connor Matthew Pautz Graham on March 16, 1995. Jim married Jenny Dyann on June 11, 1995. Their daughter, Hannah Elizabeth Graham, was born on October 18, 1999. Our circle was growing. I was care giving at both ends of the age spectrum.

It was November 22, 1995, and the day began as usual. Chuck went to his St. Paul Rotary Club, and in the afternoon, I took my mother to the doctor. She had fallen, and I wanted to make sure nothing was broken in her ankle. The doctor confirmed this, but said she shouldn't be on it much. I was concerned about the logistics of getting her help, my schedule, who to call, and other difficulties. When we got to her apartment, I tried to call Chuck at home—no cell phone then—to tell him I would be late. No answer. I called again and again. Finally I sensed something was wrong. I told my mother I would be back, and went home. Chuck was not there, and we had received no messages.

I called Rotary. "Yes, he had been there." Then the phone rang. It was our son, Jim. He said, "Mom, are you sitting down? Dad has been hit by a car while walking across Snelling Avenue. He isn't going to die, but his leg is badly injured. Also, he landed on his back and head."

I gasped and sat there, silent. Jim said, "Are you all right?"

I finally spoke to him. "Yes, I'm still able to breathe." He told me they were at the University of Minnesota Hospital, but I should wait at least ten minutes before starting to drive there. He didn't want two accident victims.

It was then something kicked in. I must have been on auto pilot. I called the St. Anthony Park block nurse who helped care for my mother and told her about the situation. She said not to worry. She would take charge of my mother's care and do what had to be done. Then I called mom's neighbor in the building, and finally, I called mom. She was very calming, assuring me that she could manage—and she did.

At the hospital I found Chuck with his leg in the air and a bandage on his head, obviously doped up, but smiling his wonderful wide grin. What a relief! Our son David soon appeared, also our minister, Reverend Tom Brennan.

Chuck had three surgeries on his leg over the next six days. Because he was on Coumadin at the time, his leg kept swelling, and the doctors could not close the wound immediately. The right side of his head also began to swell. The swelling moved down his head to his throat and he soon needed a breathing tube. At this point, he was admitted to intensive care. In spite of all of this, he rallied quickly and was in the hospital only two and one-half weeks.

During this time, I realized every hospital patient needs an advocate, another new role for me. I was constantly trying to get Chuck the help he needed. For instance, the first day out of Intensive Care, he woke up with the hiccups. The doctors and nurses all had ideas for stopping them. Some said, "Hold your breath." Others said, "Count to ten," or "Drink a glass of water at once without breathing!" I knew he was suffering.

Two hours went by. I asked his nurse to call his internist. The nurse said she couldn't do that because the orthopedists were in charge now. I knew they had already been there and had done nothing. So I figured I could call his doctor. I told the nurse I would do so, and went to the phone to make the call. As I was placing the call, she found me and said she had contacted the Internal Medicine staff. His doctor came immediately and diagnosed stomach spasms. Medication took care of it.

When Chuck came home, the fun began. He could not put any weight on his leg for four months so he used crutches, a walker, or a wheelchair. We faced some big challenges like getting from the wheelchair to a regular chair, getting in and out of the shower, our bed or the car. The second day home, Chuck fell. He wasn't hurt, but I couldn't get him up. We had to call 911. Our neighbors rushed over, and after Chuck was righted, we all had a sigh of relief, and then a good laugh.

At this point in his recovery, I realized that I needed to be home unless someone was in the house. We had lots of company, friends who would stop by for a visit. While they were there, I could sometimes sneak away for a short period of time to do errands. After another two weeks went by, I decided to go out to tend to my support group at our church, leaving Chuck alone. This support group was a volunteer project. It was organized to help members, friends, and neighbors of the church who were out of work. It included persons of all faiths from the northern suburbs of St. Paul.

The years 1989 to 1996 were times when large blocks of men and women workers from such places as UNISYS, NCR, and Honeywell were unemployed. We helped our friends recover from their anger and then look at new options. I conducted interest and values assessments. We looked at the possibility of transferring hobbies into jobs. We also rewrote resumes and conducted practice interviewing.

That day went well with the group, but as I drove down the street toward home, I couldn't believe my eyes. A fire truck and rescue squad with lights flashing sat right in front of our house! I steeled myself. I thought, "What more can happen? I failed. I shouldn't have left Chuck alone." I was afraid to go in, but when I did, I found Chuck was just fine. The cause of the trouble was a malfunctioning carbon monoxide detector. Chuck heard the signal but could do nothing, so he called

911. Once again, the neighbors collected, and since the situation wasn't serious, they agreed we kept the neighborhood lively.

Right after Christmas that year, about six weeks after Chuck's and my mother's accidents, we decided to go out to dinner. I knew a spot where I could drive up very close to the door so my patients wouldn't have to walk on the ice. Just in case it was icy, I carried a carpet along to lay down over the snow and ice so they wouldn't slip.

I think we looked like the Circus McGurkus loading and unloading from my car two "pedomically" disadvantaged souls and all their gear. My mother had a walker and Chuck needed both a wheelchair and a walker. We got along okay coming into the restaurant and getting seated, but when we went to leave, mom dropped her walker, Chuck got his wheelchair stuck under the table, and I was struggling. The man at a table near us started to laugh as he got up to help us. He was so embarrassed, but at that point we

The Graham family at Red Rock Ranch, Wyoming, 1999. Front row: Chuck, Bonnie, John; back row: David and James.

all laughed. There were many times during that winter that, for me, laughter was the only way to stay sane. It relieved the tension.

We were saved in January by a wonderful angel of a friend, Eleanor Berg. Eleanor invited us to come and stay at her place in Green Valley, Arizona, for a couple of months. Chuck was certain he could get around on his crutches if he didn't have to deal with ice and snow. From the minute we got to Arizona, he was like a new person. Since it was his left leg that was injured, he realized he could drive our rental car. Also, he was now wearing a removable cast (fastened with Velcro) so he could swim and take his injured leg along for the ride. The guys at the pool helped him get from the pool to the hot tub.

There was another benefactor in the Green Valley situation. That person was Eleanor herself. She moved in with her gentleman friend, a wonderful person named Ken. We had other River Falls, Wisconsin, friends there and one of them, Helen Wyman, coined the phrase the "River Falls Mafia." We all attended different churches on Sunday mornings, but each week after church we ate our noon meal together. We also attended concerts, took classes, and often got together socially. We were hooked. Every winter after that we tried to spend at least two months in Green Valley. In 1999, we bought our townhouse in Encanto Estates.

The years from 1996 to 1999 moved on with conflicting emotions for me. As Chuck got better, my mother went downhill. Chuck and I traveled some and tried to spend time at our cabin, but mother needed help. I pretty much gave up my counseling practice. I just couldn't do it all. Besides, I felt that the younger generation needed to work with someone closer to their age. I still help with a resume or an interview if asked.

I did join a writing group in Green Valley and have enjoyed this new effort. I also have time to swim every day or take a long walk with Chuck.

In the fall of 1999, we hit another crisis point. Jim and Jenny were expecting their first child the end of December or the first of January.

Things seemed to be going well. On about the 12th of October, we were headed out to homecoming at Champaign-Urbana, Illinois, when we heard from Jim that Jenny had been rushed to the hospital with premature labor. They tried to stop the baby, but Hannah was born on October 18, 1999. She came at twenty-six weeks, and weighed 2.9 pounds. She breathed on her own the second day. However, her condition was very fragile. At one point, she weighed only 2.2 pounds. We didn't take our trip. We stood by Jim and Jenny and tried to help when we could.

After about two weeks, we got a call from the same hospital in Minneapolis. My mother had just been taken there by ambulance. I rushed over and found her with a badly injured knee. They put her in a cast but she couldn't walk very well. Her whole body was getting weaker. She was ninety-three at the time. Mom was in one end of Abbott Northwestern Hospital and Hannah in the Neo-Natal Unit at the other. I spent my time going back and forth between them. I figured it was about two blocks, within the hospital, each way. The one thing that helped my nerves the most was my lap swimming. I tried to get to the pool as often as I could even though I didn't do much else.

Gradually, Hannah began to improve and grow. She came home from the hospital just before Christmas. My mother didn't do so well. We had to move her from her assisted living to a nursing home. She could not manage on her own anymore.

The nursing home was a horror show. The aides were inexperienced and communication between the nurses and aides was poor. I found myself training the staff on how to put on her brace properly and how to get her off the toilet. At one point, the aides let her fall while helping her dress, and she badly sprained her ankle. I despaired. We looked for a different place, but nothing seemed much better. One of mom's problems was that she was heavy and hard to move. She needed two aides each time, and most of the time only one was available—or one and me.

I could see immediately the problem with communications. My business training taught me the need for efficiency. I began to make suggestions starting with having the head nurse face her desk out toward the hall instead of the wall. That way she could see the aides and make certain they were working.

My mother died June 27, 2000, only one month short of her ninety-fourth Birthday. She had been in the nursing home six months. She wanted to live into the millennium and she did. I have thought a lot about going back to that home and tactfully trying to help them with a process that would bring about efficient and caring delivery of health care, but I can't do it yet. My bad memories are still too vivid, and after all, I am not a professional nursing home expert. I don't carry much clout. Another problem is that nursing homes in Minnesota are severely underfunded, and there is resistance to anything that would cost more money.

I miss my mother and those last ten years with her. We were almost like sisters. I still run to the phone thinking I should call her about something interesting or exciting.

After my mother died, Chuck and I once again had more time to travel, including winters in Green Valley. However, we were kept very busy at home with three more new grandchildren. Katherine Therese Pautz Graham was born October 15, 2000. She is David and Therese's third child, and sister to Andrew and Connor. Ava Nicole Graham was born to Jim and Jenny Graham on June 18, 2002. She was followed by a brother, Reid Spencer Max Graham, who arrived May 31, 2004. They join their big sister, Hannah. We see a lot of all of them in the summer at the cabin. Andrew, Connor, and Kate now live three blocks from us and attend Minnehaha Academy, which is right next door to us at Becketwood on West River Road in Minneapolis.

Our fiftieth wedding anniversary was September 2, 2001. As I might have foreseen, there was the usual unexpected turn to this event. We thought it fitting to celebrate in Duluth, my home town and favorite city, and our wedding scene fifty years ago. There are lots of things to see and do there.

Chuck and Bonnie Graham on their fiftieth wedding anniversary, Septemer 2, 2001.

When we called the Radisson Hotel in January, we asked for rooms for each family facing the lake. We checked again in May to make certain our request for lake-facing rooms was still on the books.

The day of our event in late July, Chuck and I arrived about 11:00 a.m. to make certain everything was all right. Not so. We found that only one of our rooms faced the lake. We began to negotiate for the other rooms, and produced documents stating their promise to us. They didn't move easily. It took several hours of talking and negotiating with the clerks, and finally, the manager, to get our promised rooms. We were exhausted from trying to be "Minnesota nice."

The boys and their families arrived at the hotel about 4:00 P.M. Just at that time, the fog began to roll in. It started out like puffy cotton fingers and then graduated into large moving fogbanks. We could see nothing out our window except the street ten floors below us.

The whole crowd thought the non-view of the lake was hilarious after all of our negotiations. As a former Duluthian, I should have been

155

able to predict this situation. In Duluth fog often creeps up very unexpectedly, and there is absolutely nothing you can do about it. It had been a beautiful, sunlit day.

We had arranged to have an anniversary dinner on a sightseeing boat that would go under the Aerial Bridge into Lake Superior and return to cruise the harbor. We looked at each other and said, "Now what?" Chuck called the boat company, and they assured us that they would go out but stay inside the harbor and ride alongside the docks—where they could see! The fog lifted just enough to make it easier to find the dock and see our surroundings.

The *Vista Star* held about 100 passengers. We were a party of sixteen. Kate was the youngest at one year. Lindsay, our oldest grandchild, was seventeen. There were eight grandchildren with us and eight adults. The boat crew had decorated our tables in blue and white as we requested. It was very festive!

Our waiters that night were personable, happy, genuinely interested young men, mostly college students. They asked us when we would like the champagne. We were startled. We had been given the choice between a cake and champagne, and we chose the cake because of the children. We explained this to them. They looked stricken. They didn't have a cake. There must have been a mix-up. We assured them it would be okay. We didn't want an incident to spoil our fun, so we asked them to give the adults the champagne and provide soft drinks for the kids.

After dinner the grandchildren spread around the boat to see what they could see in the fog. The nice captain invited them up, two at a time, to sit with him and help him steer.

All of a sudden one of them spotted a little motor boat with one driver. The boat was bobbing and tossing up and down in the choppy bay. Our grandson shouted out, and we all ran to the side to see what crazy person was out in a boat in such bad weather.

The little boat kept bobbing around. Then, it began to come closer. By now most of the passengers were watching. Suddenly, it came up to the side of our boat. Our crew reached down and, between the driver and themselves, managed to transfer a large package to our deck.

Lo and behold, it contained a very beautifully decorated anniversary cake! We were nearing the Wisconsin side of the harbor, and the cake was made in a Superior, Wisconsin, bakery. The bakery recruited a very brave boater to deliver it to us. Our young waiters had arranged for all of this. They grinned like Cheshire cats. The whole ship cheered. What a party! We ate the cake and celebrated together. This was a special day we will never forget.

We made the decision in the spring of 2005 to leave our big home in Roseville and move into a condo. We didn't want to keep up our house along with the cabin and our town house in Arizona. We moved into Becketwood Co-op in August 2005. It has been a good move for us. We are located on the Mississippi River with a lovely view. There are miles of walkway along the drive, and we can get out regularly.

Since my mother's death and our retirement, I have been thinking of my role as a woman spanning these past fifty years. I experienced practical feminism during the 1950s. I would define this as carrying out the proscribed role that was assigned to us to live from day to day. This would include taking a paid job if it was absolutely necessary, child care, the need to please our husbands or maintain our role in society, and, for a single woman, taking a job to pay the bills.

Then in the 1960s we seemed to move in the opposite direction to what I would call fantasy feminism. At that time Betty Friedan popularized the word feminism, which is defined as the theory of the political, economic and social equality of the sexes. Many of the young women I counseled in the 1970s and 1980s wanted it all!—marriage, full-time professional careers and motherhood. They would not consider that they might have to make choices along the way. Part of this thinking was unrealistic.

In the 1990s I again worked with some of the same women who were looking to be less tied to their jobs so they could spend more time with their children or take care of aging parents or other new circumstances. Two of my professional daughters-in-law are now running their own businesses from their homes, and one is teaching at a nearby college. They often have the same vacation time as their children. They are now able to be there for their kids. Of course not all women can do this, but many today try to work out a compromise schedule of some sort.

It seems to me that today we have a form of reality feminism which I define as two people or a single parent working long hard hours to keep the family financially afloat—not abandoning family values but still wanting to be free to follow a chosen career path. A vast majority of women manage this dual role well but they are torn in their loyalties between husband, family, work, and a host of other interests in their lives. It is difficult for many of them. They are constantly facing tough decisions. Single women also find it hard to maintain their many roles in society.

What we need today is to respect women's wishes and decisions no matter how they organize their lives. Instead of women asking, "What does society want of us?" we should be asking ourselves "What can we (society) do to support the choices our young and older women make?" This would help put "reality" into reality feminism.

In contemplating "what next?" in my life I am haunted by the admonition of John Wesley, founder of Methodism, who gave these instructions to his followers:

> "Do all the good you can, by all the means you can,
> In all the ways you can, in all the places you can,
> At all the times you can, to all the people you can,
> As long as ever you can."

I have tried to carry out his admonitions all my life. What he preached is the social gospel that we must take care of each other, and I agree with him. But I ask myself, when is there time for myself? Is it a sin to back off of projects and committees to spend time writing and reading?

A year or so after my mother's death, several friends said to me, "Now Bonnie, what are you going to do? What project will you tackle next?" When I said that I wasn't looking for a project, they said, "But you need to use your talents!" Do I? Couldn't I use my talents in another direction rather than social work or organizing—maybe in the arts?

A few years ago, I wrote an essay, "For What Purpose—Art?" In it I describe a person visiting us in Green Valley who did not seem happy to be there. We tried to cheer him by talking about the positive things we were doing and especially mentioned our writing class, thinking he might be interested in something like that.

The next day we had a reunion and a group of university friends joined us for lunch. In the course of the conversation, I mentioned the Arts and Craft Show at West Center. I explained to our visitors how many folks in Green Valley spend their time in various shops, making clay, working with silver, woodworking, painting with water colors or oil, and many other hands-on activities. One of our friends told how many residents are studying something or trying to express themselves through writing. Our friend stood up, waved his hands about as if to survey the scene and said, "All of this art. For what purpose?"

I was stunned! I had thought about this question often but have never been confronted with it or had to answer it on the. spot. To put it another way, "Why are we all working so hard at these various leisure activities?" I gave a fumbling answer which included being creative and releasing pent-up energy and desires, but it didn't begin to cover the subject. The topic was quickly changed.

However, these thoughts about our leisure activities come up every time someone asks me what I am doing now that I am retired. I tell them that from time to time I work as a volunteer in our church helping those who are out of work cope with their situations and find new jobs. That seems to satisfy the questioners. But if I only mention my writing interest, my interest in American Indian art, or my love of reading and swimming, they look away or ask, "What else are you doing?" This I interpret as, "What are you doing that is useful?"

Facing a question like this, we Methodists, and many others in the work ethic traditions, can start to feel hedonistic or even guilty. We begin to question our motives. We worry about John Wesley and his directive. And with this in mind we might ask ourselves, "Is this the way I should be spending my time?" For what purpose am I participating in an art or writing class—what purpose art?

Many would argue that art doesn't need a purpose. It stands alone. But, hands-on art of all kinds is a form of expression. We know doctors, lawyers, teachers, and people from all walks of life participating in various art forms. They tell me that they feel emotional release, elation or even a sense of fun! For some of us we are finally able to let the cat out of bag. What we don't always realize is that our efforts are leaving a trail behind that tells the world who we are and how we feel at this particular place in time.

So what purpose—all of this? The answer is to be found among my friends in my writing class and Chuck's pals in the Becketwood workshop. Of course, we take time to help our neighbors and others in need, but we also make time for our art—for our own self-expression. I like to think generations to come will benefit from my friends' efforts and from mine. Hopefully, we will join the ranks of painters, musicians, potters and writers whose messages still enlighten us today.

During these past fifty plus years, I have lived and loved and enjoyed. From my early education in Duluth, Minnesota, to the University of Illinois in Urbana, and the University of Wisconsin-Whitewater, I have had experiences that equipped me to think and rethink the many situations and cultures I confronted along my life's journey.

My children and grandchildren have been a constant source of inspiration and wonder. My husband has been a supporting rock for me.

We have caring friends both here at home and all over the world. The cultural differences among them have been stimulating and challenging. From all of them I have learned and grown as a woman. I am grateful.

The extended Graham clan in 2008. Front circle: Granddaughter Lindsay and her husband, Kevin Bourgo; Left to right: front row: Jenny Graham, Ava Graham, Hannah Graham, Bonnie and Chuck Graham, and Connor Graham; middle row: Therese Pautz, David Graham, Martha Morris Graham, Benjamin Graham, Jim (James) Graham holding Reid Graham and Andrew Graham; top row: John Graham holding Kate Graham, Matthew Graham, and David Graham.